AHOBOBO

On the Sacramental Imagination in West Africa

Bénin, 2006–2008

Yanick St. Jean

University Press of America,® Inc.

Lanham · Boulder · New York · Toronto · Plymouth, UK

Copyright © 2011 by
University Press of America,® Inc.
4501 Forbes Boulevard
Suite 200
Lanham, Maryland 20706
UPA Acquisitions Department (301) 459-3366

Estover Road
Plymouth PL6 7PY
United Kingdom

Library of Congress Control Number: 2010937546
ISBN: 978-0-7618-5365-7 (paperback : alk. paper)
eISBN: 978-0-7618-5366-4

Front cover image: Porte du non retour

⊖™ The paper used in this publication meets the minimum
requirements of American National Standard for Information
Sciences—Permanence of Paper for Printed Library Materials,
ANSI Z39.48-1992

To the memory of Ralph
transformed into new life while I was in Benin.

To my students at the *Institut Jean Paul II* and the *University of Abomey Calavi.*

To my children and grandchildren, dearest people in my life.

Contents

Acknowledgements

September 1, 2006. Just after 7:05 p.m., bright lights twinkle in the dark of the night. We've just landed at the *Aéroport International de Cotonou* (Cotonou's international airport). Standing behind fellow passengers and ready for the unbelievable experience, I await my turn outside the door. A wave of heat tells me the summer clothes I wear are much too thick. I do not remember experiencing this kind of heat so deep under my skin.

In the backdrop are sounds of drums mixed with instruments I hardly recognize. But the rhythms, I remember from Haiti. I have a strong desire to kiss the ground. As other passengers, I proceed toward the building through immigration then another room. A crowd of people surrounds the belt, some awaiting bags, others hoping for incoming passengers needing transportation. Motor-taxi conductors wearing bright yellow shirts announce their *zemijans*. Looking around, I think I am in Haiti. I continue hearing and seeing familiar and not-so-familiar sounds and sites. I am more focused on what is around me than on the arrival of my luggage. This mixture of people was a prelude and analogy to the mixture of faiths I was about to uncover.

A man holding a sign bearing my name identifies himself as Eric, staff member of the American Cultural Center. I breathe deeply. Eric and Public Affairs Officer John Cushing waiting outside, have come to meet me and take me to the *Chant d'Oiseau*, a hostel for several weeks that would be my home. Soon after Eric's greeting, my three suitcases holding mostly research equipment, health items and enough clothing for a couple of weeks make their appearance on the belt. They are rolled out (no help from me) to the front of the building. On the way out, someone tries to stop me. I recall Eric's authoritative voice and command: *Laissez-la passer*. That takes care of that.

Outside the building, PAO John Cushing greets me and makes sure I do not need anything immediately. He offers to pick me up the next morning if needed, to show the city, and help exchange into Beninese currency (*CFA communauté financière africaine*) the fewer than three-hundred American dollars in my pocket. About 10 minutes later, we arrive at the hostel. Three flights of stairs and I enter a clean, ventilated, rectangular room with mosquito-netted beds, bright color sheets, a small table and an eye-catching bathroom—no hot water.

I must have slept a little but the drums did not, for I still hear them in the dawn, muffled by chanting of Muslims and, later, voices of nuns reciting their Divine Office in a nearby chapel. *A fon ganji a*, (bonjour) Bénin! Research on the sacramental imagination, the issue of diversity, and similarities among diaspora people has taken me far across the world. A new life that would last two academic years is just starting.

This research began in the United States Midwest as intellectual inquiry about the sacramental imagination would continue in the former Dahomey as both an intellectual and personal journey. I grew up in Haiti the youngest of four children. My father went to Mass in the morning and we attended Catholic schools. I grew up afraid of Vodou, of Vodou rhythms, of the word Vodou, and anything or anyone associated with it. As I look back, it seems the mission of these schools was that of rearing 'good French women.' I did not fit the setting—except for constant fear . . . the fear of Vodou.

In the United States, I was flooded with questions about Vodou, as if Haitian were synonymous with it. Sometimes I resented what appeared to me an overgeneralization, given my general lack of understanding of the practice. Other times, I thought it helpful to be knowledgeable, in case questions kept coming. Most times however, fear prevailed. I usually avoided the topic altogether or as much as I could. But, avoidance proves difficult in an academic setting. It proved difficult in Benin. I came to Benin to interview Catholics—Catholics only, but the complexity of the field took me in a different direction more inclusive—as I found it necessary to study non-Catholics as well. This decision followed careful observation and preliminary interviews that signaled the convoluted nature of the Catholic imagination. The benefits of this work are only too obvious. The borders of the sacramental imagination are porous and, especially in Benin where everything is negotiated, religious immigration, emigration and reverse migration are challenging at best to observe, explain, and predict.

In the pages that follow, the people speak about their faiths in their own language and style. I tried preserving naturalness even as many quotes are translated from their original French. The people speak for themselves so that in the absence of direct access, readers can see the words uttered by these voices and make their own interpretations. This is part of the joy in qualitative analysis.

Ahobobo in the title may sound strange to the western ear. But *Ahobobo* is at the intersection of the Catholic and traditional imaginations. It symbolizes the occasional exchange from one to the other. *Ahobobo* is sometimes shouted during or after Catholic songs. One example is the Catholic liturgical *Kilisu* (Christ in *fon-gbe*, the language of the Fon people). But Ahobobo is also of interest because close to *Abobo* according to Alfred Métraux (1959: 325) expresses religious enthusiasm in Haitian Vaudou. "L'exclamation est accompagnée parfois du bruit que l'on produit en frappant la bouche avec les doigts [occasionally, the exclamation accompanies the noise produced by tapping the mouth with fingers]. The same noise is produced in Benin. There is also *Ayibobo*, a popular cry of enthusiasm in Haiti. So I thought *Ahobobo* a good representation of the link between Beninese Catholicism, and between West Africa and the diaspora.

I never dreamed of going to Africa. Thanks to the Fulbright staff in Washington D.C., to Valerie Gilpin, but especially Debra Egan, for guidance and patience during and after I applied for the fellowship. A very special thanks to Joe Feagin who has inspired me since my years as a graduate student at the University of Texas. Thanks to Andrew Greeley whom I never met, but whose ideas bring a ray of sunshine to the dark world of racial inequality. Thanks also to colleagues and friends in big and small ways contributed to this effort—Fay Akindes, Taïbatou Osséni, Alberta Bailey, Valerie Hunt, Ania Zajicek, Père Charles Agbessi, Père Raymond Goudjo, Père Théophile Akoa, Professeur Honorat Aguéssy, Pierre Métinhoué, Jean Plyat, Pasteur Sambieni, Bob Fadegnon, Père AdéÉdouard, Franck Ogou, Alain Godonou, Gabin Adjanon, Nathanaël Totin, Brice Sacramento, Robert Mnshimiyimana, Fortunée Moganou, Jean-Olivier Chéou, Pédro Marius Égounleti, and especially, Alain Godonou, Gérard Tognimassou, Père Philippe Kinkpon. While trying to develop a list of people to acknowledge, I found it too long yet incomplete. Dr. Steven Worden offered valuable comments and ideas that help to strengthen an earlier version of the manuscript. No matter how carefully prepared such a list I am bound to leave out someone. So thanks to all and to many who helped with this work—recommended articles and books, shared insights, accompanied me from city to city, village to village, city to village, taught me *fon-gbe*, invited me into their homes, to religious ceremonies, treated my malaria and other ills with *coca-cola* (and medications, of course), shopped with me at *Marché D'Anktopa*, designed my clothes, braided my hair, made me *amiyo*, *igname pilé*, *bissap*, taught me to fold a *pagne*, danced with me, all who stressed a positive outlook on life . . . The list goes on . . . and on. You know who you are.

For love, prayers and support, I thank my daughters, Claudia, Chantal and Stephanie. A special thanks to Stephanie who stood in for me and was diligent in making sure everything went smoothly during my two-year absence from the United States. I could not have done this without you!

From the Beninese treasure I gathered mounds. Yet, more would have been, were I initiated into traditional religion. Due to respect for my African ancestors and the people who practice, I would not want initiation for the sole purpose of fact-finding.

Yanick St. Jean,
January 2010

Chapter One
Divine-in-the-World[1]

*I would like to have schools for
the Vodun religion that use the same principle as Catholic schools because Catholic
schools are so good and so successful*
(Dignitary of traditional religion)

[Les écoles Catholiques?] Ah, c'est une bonne chose. Mon souhait maintenant .
. . j'aimerais (c'est un message que je dois ajouter à votre question) . . . nous
aimerions aussi que cette école là soit aussi créée au niveau de notre tradition
pour que nos nouveaux adeptes qui sortent du couvent aillent à l'école, pour
que demain nous ayons des cadres dans nos couvents, puisque si les
missionnaires, ou bien les Islams, n'avaient pas créé leurs écoles il ne pourrait
pas avoir de cadres chez nous. Beaucoup de cadres de ce pays sont passés par
là. C'est pourquoi, nous, notre souhait, moi mon grand chantier c'est que je
dois tout faire et je vais tout faire, je vais toujours prier pour que l'école des
adeptes voit le jour. Donc vous avez bien posé la question, si l'école des
missionnaires est une bonne chose. Nous voulons aussi que l'école des *vodúnsì*
connaisse le jour.

[Ah, Catholic schools are a good thing. My wish now . . . I would like (and it is
a message that I have to add to your question) . . . we would like also that this
school be also created at the level of our tradition so that our new adepts who
are coming out of the convent go to school, so that tomorrow we may have professionals in our convents, because if missionaries, or Muslims, had not created
their schools, we would not have professionals. Many professionals in this
country have passed through there. That is why, we . . . our wish, my big building site, is that I must do everything and I will do everything, I am going to
pray so that the school of adepts sees the light. So, you have posed the question
well, if the schools of missionaries are a good thing. We too would like that the
school of Vodun sees the day].

The opening words are those of a high dignitary of traditional (Vodun) religion
whom I interviewed at his residence in southern Benin. Though not a follower of

the Catholic faith, he recognizes something special in the Catholic educational system where he himself was trained at an early age. He wishes to model the experience and to shape his own traditional schools so they too may be as successful, but only in a traditional sense.

I chose this particular statement by the dignitary to show, while the present research uses Catholicism as its case study, the idea guiding it is much broader. The *Daah* (title used for Vodun priests) [2] wanted to borrow the idea of religious schools, hoping to implement it, thereby strengthen traditional (Vodun) identity. This work is similar in its attempts to understand the Beninese Catholic imagination and to discover its nature particularly in relation to diversity. What is the face of Catholicism in Benin? Is the Beninese Catholic imagination open to diversity and social justice? What lesson (s) to be learned, perhaps serve as a model for other popular (or religious) imaginations? Finally, could the presence or absence of a Catholic imagination account for different preferences observed in African diasporic cultures? But first I explain the meaning of Catholic imagination and lay out the story behind these questions, how the study came to be, and the motivations for it that have raised an immense amount of curiosity among both colleagues and respondents.

In the United States, whenever I share that I am studying the Catholic imagination, the recent priest sex abuse scandal and the decline of the American priesthood are raised almost immediately. Never once did these issues surface in West Africa where time after time, I was reminded that the study is important. West African theologians have reflected on Catholicism but, say, the Catholic imagination has not been sufficiently studied sociologically. The concern with priestly sex abuse is typically American, consistent with the direction of media focus in the United States. However, both in the United States and West Africa, I am asked often 1) what Catholic imagination means and 2) how the idea for the study originated. In what follows, I address these two queries.

What Catholic imagination means

Definitions are often arbitrary. They vary depending upon who defines and the power of the definer. More problematic are boundaries definitions set, boundaries that blind us to important sources of information. Here I cite as an example the Protestant Theologian David Cox who, on the difficulty of definitions regarding theological topics, writes "the current theological language does not provide adequate categories and terms for the discussion of perseverance, assurance and the warning passages" (Cox, 2006: 8). The Catholic imagination is not exempt from definitional difficulties. "To attempt a definition of religion is an almost impossible, if not altogether impossible, task; and every serious scholar is on the verge of giving up the task" (Idowu, 1973: 69). Yet conceptual definitions are essential.

One definition of the Catholic imagination is seeing the sacred in the profane. [3] This definition suggests no limits to the sacred. Yet, Émile Durkheim (as stated in Lukes, 1972: 24) distinguishes between sacred and profane. "Sacred things are those which the interdiction protect and isolate; profane things, those to which these interdictions are applied and which must remain at a distance from the first" (Durkheim as stated in Lukes, 1972: 25).

> In all the history of human thought, there exists no other example of two categories of things so profoundly differentiated, so radically opposed to one another . . . the sacred and the profane have always and everywhere been conceived by the human mind as separate classes, as two worlds between which there is nothing in common.

In light of the Durkheimian distinction, defining the Catholic imagination as "seeing the sacred in the profane," appears revolutionary and transgresses traditional conceptual boundaries. However, a more careful look reveals seeing the sacred in the profane is different from the merging of sacred and profane. Seeing the sacred in the profane suggests an open mind looking deeply into the profane for the sacred.

Unlike Durkheim, Max Weber did not provide a definition of religion but meaning can be derived from his work. For Weber, religion is a source of social change. Religion "governs relations." Weber's charisma is Durkheim's sacred for « [l]e charisme est la qualité de ce qui est comme dit Max Weber hors du quotidien (ausseralltäglich) » (Cipriani, 2004: 127) [charisma is a quality of what is, as Max Weber puts it, outside the everyday]. For Weber thus, the Catholic imagination (as other religious imaginations) would govern relations in daily life and by "enchanting" mentalities, contribute to social change.

Another definition of Catholic imagination is "seeing the invisible in the visible." The visible are images, symbols, rites, and experience that link a believer to 1) other believers; 2) a community of believers; and 3) the invisible. The Catholic imagination builds from the visible to represent the invisible. Believers' creative vision of the world guides their approach to everyday life (Cipriani, 2004).

In sum, the Catholic imagination refers to a "Catholic viewpoint that God is present in the whole creation and in human beings, as seen in its sacramental system whereby material things and human beings are channels and sources of God's grace" (see *Wikipedia* internet source). The sociologist-priest Andrew Greeley (2000) who popularized the concept uses the example of a sandwich.

If someone you love prepares a sandwich for you, it acquires meaning beyond two slices of bread (the material) because inhabited by something that you, the receiver, consider love (nonmaterial). "Something else" makes this sandwich special, transforms it, enchants it, as the receiver's imagination travels beyond visibility. The sandwich becomes one of the transformed "material things" that "are channels and sources of God's grace." I am reminded here of a comment by an interviewee that "everything is grace." Grace suggests the presence of a divine mingling in everything and everywhere. Grace suggests a divine-in-the-world. "Everything is grace" and divine-in-the world come close to the idea of the Catholic imagination.

The theme "divine-in-the-world" or "God in the world" are found in both definitions. The themes are also found over and over in the writings of Ignatius of Loyola, for example when he writes (see Guiliani, 1997: 206).[4]

> Le but des études ne permet pas aux scolastiques de longues méditations. C'est pourquoi, en dehors des exercices qu'ils ont pour la vertu (entendre la messe chaque jour, consacrer une heure à l'oraison et à l'examen de conscience, se confesser et communier chaque semaine), ils peuvent s'éxercer à chercher la présence de Notre Seigneur en toutes choses, par exemple dans les conversations, en allant et venant, en tout ce qu'ils voient, goûtent, entendent, comprennent, et en tout ce qu'ils peuvent faire. Car il est vrai que sa divine Majesté est, par sa présence, sa puissance et son essence, en toutes choses. Et cette manière de méditer, trouvant Dieu notre Seigneur en toutes choses, est plus facile que de s'élever aux choses divines plus abstraites par un effort pour s'y rendre présent.

> [Their studies do not allow scholars to engage in long meditations. That is why, outside of exercises they have for virtue (attend Mass everyday, allow one hour to prayer and examination of conscience, confess and take communion each week), they can practice looking for the presence of Our Lord in all things, for example in conversations, going and coming, in all that they see, taste, hear, understand, and in all that they can do. For it is true that the divine Majesty is, by its presence, its power and its essence, in everything. And this form of meditation, finding God our Lord in everything, is easier than to rise to more abstract divine things with effort so that one can be present].

For St. Ignatius, one must "'trouver Dieu' au sein de l'action la plus absorbante" [find God' in the midst of the most abundant action] (Giuliani, 1997: 208). Everything is prayer. "Dans l'action et dans l'étude, on peut porter son esprit vers Dieu; et quand on dirige tout vers le service de Dieu, tout est oraison" [in action and in study, one can carry his spirit to God, and when one directs everything toward the service of God, everything is prayer] (Loyola as stated in Guiliani, 1997: 208).

All of this suggests that Catholics live in a world they perceive to be "haunted" by a spirit—a holy spirit (Greeley, 2000). Believers stretch their imaginations to represent to themselves this hidden reality. Sacraments (baptism, communion, reconciliation, confirmation, marriage, sacrament of the sick, holy orders) and sacramentals (candles, blessed water, statues, novenas, rosaries, picture images, relics, incense, gregorian chants, other religious songs)—all part of the collective memory of Catholic Christianity move the intellect closer to this world-haunting spirit. So do foods, objects, and other trivial of everyday life. For example, to the extent that the sandwich (a food, material and visible) prepared by someone else is a metaphor for love (non-material and invisible) it too would move the intellect beyond the immediate (visible and material) closer to this world-haunting spirit (invisible and non-material) for the sandwich (visible and material) is enchanted.

Comparable sources of enchantment in secular everyday life include baby clothes that mothers keep after their children have grown. The other day, my granddaughter Charlotte, six years of age, opened her closet and proudly showed me dresses now too small but neatly arranged in hangers, and still taking up space. "Mommy does not want to get rid of them," she said to me. This, I find another example of enchantment in everyday life—the material that has become non-material. Other similar sources of enchantment are old letters from family and friends, picture albums (all connectors to the invisible and non-material). No matter how old, these keepsakes may never be exchanged or discarded. Imagination travels beyond these immediate "things," beyond visibleness into their invisibleness. They become part of a memory that marks a period of time—usually a happy one. So it is in the Catholic imagination where the world is a metaphor for God (see Greeley 2000; 1989). The material world is transformed into a non-material and tells us something about the invisible.

The Catholic imagination is only one of many religious imaginations. Religious imaginations perceive something "out there" to be much bigger than what the intellect can capture. Religious imaginations may be Christian, Muslim, Protestant (or dialectical),[5] Animist, Vodun.[6] Yet, different religions will capture differently the hidden in the physical world. For Christian Catholics, the world-haunting Holy Spirit is not visible to the naked eye. Thus, symbols help stretch the believers' imaginations so they may represent to themselves this "roaming" spirit reality. Particular signs and symbols shape a particular sensibility and a particular practice of everyday life. Signs and symbols build a shared sensibility and a community. Through interaction, they enhance the experience of rituals.

On symbols and rituals.

Émile Durkheim (as cited in Lukes, 1972: 463) thought that,

> 'after a collective effervescence men believe themselves transported into an entirely different world from the one they have before their eyes,' that sacred beings, the creations of collective thought, 'attain their greatest intensity at the moment when the men are assembled together and are in immediate relations with one another, when they all partake of the same idea and the same sentiment.'

Durkheim (as cited in Lukes, 1972: 466) saw religion as

> 'a system of ideas with which the individuals represent to themselves the society of which they are members, and the obscure but intimate relations which they have with it'; [that] 'the sacred principle,' he maintained, is nothing more or less than society hypostasized and transfigured', and he argued that religion

'reflects all [society's] aspects, even the most vulgar and the most repulsive.
All is to be found there.'

These words bring to mind 1871, the year of the religious ceremony at *Bois Caïman*.[7] Myth or reality, this historical event is engraved in the Haitian national memory. According to historical reports, just before the Haitian Revolution, the African enslaved, who wanted freedom from their chains gathered for a religious (Vodou) ceremony at a place called Bois Caïman. It is here, at this very gathering that was produced the force and excitement, the enthusiasm which led eventually to the defeat of Napoleon's troops and the Independence of Haïti. The enslaved gathered for this ceremony shared a collective memory of religion. They were "assembled together," "in immediate relations with one another," and "they all [were] partake[ing] of the same idea and the same sentiment." They wanted to be freed from servitude.[8] They invoked their African gods. They found strength in their religion.

Even if these enslaved were not from the same tribe they shared a collective memory of place and religion. They were transported through their imaginations and through the excitement of rituals to an invisible world, an "entirely different world from the one they ha[d] before their eyes."

What point is being made? Though the essential functions of sacraments and sacramentals differ in levels of importance, sacraments and sacramentals are otherwise similar in their function as connectors of the visible to the invisible. They can be a source of social change. The forms these connectors take depend upon the socio-historical-cultural context.

Catholicism tends to absorb the surrounding culture with its ethnic flavors. Irish Catholicism is different from the Italian, Polish, German, Mexican, and French versions. . . . [In the United States] how Italians, Germans, Mexicans, French, and Tarahumara Indians practice Catholicism informs us about their ethnicities" (See St. Jean 2007: 158).

If being open to diversity (racial or otherwise) is an essential part of Catholic identity, this value would be reflected one way or another in different Catholic imaginations both at the individual and collective levels. The more tolerant a society, the more open to diversity would be its Catholic population. Durkheim (Lukes, 1972: 466) 'argued that religion 'reflects all [society's] aspects, even the most vulgar and the most repulsive. All is to be found there,' including the noble.[9]

Pierre Bourdieu might have called this collective memory a "religious habitus" or "religious capital." Though Bourdieu rooted his habitus in conditions of class, Terry Rey builds on Bourdieu's concept to include "identity linked to race, gender, ethnicity and religion" (Rey, 2005: 455). It is Rey's addition of ethnicity and religion as habitus and his focus on a collective level which is of particular interest here. Rey noted the potential impact of religious capital on society already evident in Durkheim's study of suicide in Europe, and Max Weber's study of religion and capitalism (Rey, 2006). Borrowing from Rey, we see the ceremony at Bois Caïman as example of integration in a shared religious capital impacting[10] religious enthusiasm and acting as a force for social change. Further, Bois Caïman shows the force of religious integration on social action. The Civil Rights movement of the 1960s provides another example of religious enthusiasm and the resulting force in favor of social change.

While much can be learned from Bois Caïman and the Civil Rights movement about religious imaginations and collective memories as catalysts for action, this work is neither specifically about Bois Caïman nor about Animism of which Vodou is one form.[11] This work is about lived Catholic imagination (catholicisme vécu,)[12] habitus, religious capital, or collective memory. I use the example of Bois Caïman because it illustrates well the sense of community and action that can follow from religious enthusiasm.

For Catholics, believing firmly in a "haunted world and that "everything is grace" should impact rituals and the actions of believers in everyday life, especially when "assembled" and "partaking in the same idea and sentiment." As in the case of Bois Caïman, common religious rituals and beliefs build community. In everyday life, intense religious exultation during rituals can lead to the building of a religious capital both at the individual and collective levels. Durkheim noted the communitarian character of Catholicism in his study of suicide in Europe, and so did Weber in analyzing the influence of religious ideas on the economy.

Following Bois Caïman, Haïti had the only known successful slave insurrection led first by General Toussaint L'Ouverture and after the French captured Toussaint, Jean-Jacques Dessalines. To understand Bois Caïman and its impact on the enslaved, it is necessary first to understand the popular imagination (lived Vodouism) which guided their actions, and the importance of shared values (including freedom) that were being asserted. In this context, one question for research might be "What can be learned from the Bois Caïman event about the Vodou [animist (sic)] imagination?" What is the meaning of a Vodou imagination? And more importantly, what are the implications of a Vodou imagination for social justice?

Previous research demonstrates that American Catholics are more likely to oppose racism than other Americans. Catholic congregations are less racially segregated than others. "Here comes everybody" is James Joyce's vision of Catholicism. To understand more clearly Catholicism's impact on diversity (Greeley's research, de Tocqueville), it is necessary to study different Catholic contexts or constructions, to identify patterns that may link one context to the other and impact the faithful in a certain way.

A baby blanket woven and sewn in a particular culture adopts its character. A recipe depends upon local ingredients. In the area of religion, communion hosts usually round and flat, are not so everywhere. Gifts brought to the altar during Mass—usually in the form of money—could also be breads, fruits and vegetables. A priest's chasuble may be plain cloth or in some churches, *pagne* (African) fabric. The popularity of a saint depends upon each culture. In Benin, St. Pio (also known as Padre Pio) and Ste Thérèse de Lisieux are popular. Devotion to Mary may more or less, depending upon a culture. In Benin, the faithful sing to Mary at the end of every Mass. Mexican Americans venerate Our Lady of Guadalupe more so than Anglo Americans. Mary adopts the face and features of each culture.

But first and foremost, blankets protect from cold—their main function. Regardless of recipe, food is for consumption. Money, breads, fruits, vegetables, or something else offered during Mass are gifts from the faithful. For Catholics, consecrated hosts in whatever shape or texture are transubstantiated into the body of Christ. The meaning of a chasuble does not vary with the cloth from which it is made. Finally, regardless of cultural representation and whether she is Marie, Mary, Maria, or Malia (in *fon-gbe*), for the faithful, this icon is a powerful figure model of womanhood and mother who can intercede to a higher power (her son).

When I use the term Catholic imagination I mean popular Catholicism in everyday life. As one respondent comments, "The Catholic imagination is constructed from what can be found in the immediate surrounding." So, the Catholic imagination is how in a particular society, people feel, live, build their Catholicism every day. It is the people's Catholicism.

How the idea for the study originated

How does a researcher go from studying racism to a study of the Catholic imagination? This apparent intellectual stretch or better yet switch, is much easier to explain than the concept Catholic imagination itself.

A few years ago, while perusing the work of Andrew Greeley, I came across the idea that American Catholics are communitarian and open to diversity. This finding was important because analyses of interviews with middle-class African American men and women reveal their experience with racial discrimination and modern racism alive, still impacting their quality of life (see Feagin, 2000; Bonilla-Silva, 2006; Benjamin, 2006; Rockquemore, 2007). It was also important because of my own interviews with African American women and intermarried couples who shared similar experiences (see St. Jean and Feagin 1998; St. Jean 1994; St. Jean and Parker 1994).

While religion can "make prejudice," it can also "unmake prejudice" (Allport, 1954: 447). Jacques Maritain (1958) accents religion's role in the unmaking of prejudice: "no decisive victory . . . can be achieved without profound inner changes caused by the power of spiritual energies. In this regard the role played by the religious organizations is crucial and so is their responsibility." Historian Scott Appleby (2000: 841) observed that religion served haters and hated—each seeing God on its side—but also religion's strategic role as "powerful medicine" that can contribute consistently to peace building. Religion also appears to mediate the negative health effects of racial discrimination. As Alix Bierman (2006: 562) puts it "[g]iven the continued pervasive effect of discrimination in current [American] society, it is undoubtedly a worthy task for researchers to identify more clearly how and why religion has these [buffering] effects." Religion, in this case Catholicism, is a valuable tool for research.

Catholicism appears to have an impact on acceptance of the economic and racial other in the United States. For example, though eleven o'clock Sunday morning is said the most segregated time in the United States[13] Catholic churches are less so. American Catholics are more likely than other non-Catholic Christians to belong to interracial churches (Emerson, 2006). Long ago, Alexis de Tocqueville already recognized these differences. Thus, I decided to investigate the nature of Catholicism in everyday life to discover themes that might indicate a pattern, and help discover if Catholicism has these tolerance effects on the faithful. I decided to speak to the people themselves. This work grows out of previous research. It is an offshoot of previous work on racial and ethnic relations and racism.

While developed societies are said increasingly secularized, the importance of religion is rising in other parts of the world, particularly Africa. West Africa, which includes Benin, is an appropriate space for this study the Catholic imagination, its impact on acceptance of the other, and religious differences within diasporic cultures.

Previous research.

What impact has the Catholic imagination on antiracism, was the original question of interest. I was intrigued by Andrew Greeley's suggestion, based upon quantitative analysis, that Catholics are more likely to oppose racism than other Americans. With this in mind, I interviewed over one-hundred self-identified Catholics in the Midwest about their vision of the world and their attitude towards various racial issues including intermarriage. Most interviewees were Euro Americans but there were also some African Americans and first-generation Haitian Americans. Haitian American and African American have two separate identities. While piecing these groups into one category would help simplification, for historical and cultural reasons most Haitian Americans prefer the association with Haiti and Haitian American identity. The exact location of the interviews is not revealed due to the small size of the sample.

A majority of EuroAmerican respondents seemed open to the idea of racial intermarriage, an accepted indicator of openness.[14] While some expressed concern for the well-being of the couple and their children, almost all had such a marriage in their family. The respondents noted relatives not entirely accepting at first, but an increase in acceptance once the couple had children. It appears from this research that some Euro American Catholics in the Midwest are open to the idea of racial diversity through marriage.

The African American respondents were not against the idea of interracial marriage. They too had such marriages in their families. However, they were concerned about the couple's experience within society. Their preference was marital endogamy. They wished to preserve their ethnicity by marrying within the African American community. Most European American or African American respondents were concerned that the couple might experience additional problems due to pressure from a society where intermarriage did not become legal until the late 60's. Thus race is reflected in the imagination of this Midwestern sample. A collective memory of history interacts with and shapes the Midwestern imagination which "'reflects all [society's] aspects, even the most vulgar and the most repulsive. All is to be found there'" (Lukes, 1972: 466).

For first generation Haitian Americans, race was not a primary concern. One reason may be their association with a different historical memory. Most having arrived in the United States after 1960 were not directly affected by, thus may not relate to, *Loving vs. Virginia*, the 1967 Supreme Court case which legalized interracial marriage in the United States. Another difference with African Americans and European Americans is the awareness of the impact of Vaudou on Haitian life and practice of Catholicism. Two Haitian American respondents spoke at length about this issue.

> That what makes the Catholicism, as practiced by the Haitians . . . . imperfect, somewhat adulterated, because it is tainted by the fundamental knowledge in the culture, that fundamental nature of the culture, that fundamental element.

I became interested in explaining some religious differences between Haitian Americans and African Americans that emerged in the data, for example preference for priests who spoke their language and understood their cultures well, and different emphases on Vaudou identity. I reasoned that the source—West Africa and Benin in particular—would help in this regard. "Benin was one of the most important sources of slaves for the Americas, and perhaps for a few decades in the early eighteenth century, the ports of the Slave Coast exported more slaves than any other comparable stretch of the African shore" (Lovejoy, 1994: 328). Melville Herskovits writes: "In Haiti, also, the study of the survival of Africanisms may be profitably pursued. In this island the evidence points to Dahomey [today's Benin] as the principal source of its Negro culture (Herskovits, 1933: 259). Continues Herskovits (1933: 262),

> Generalized West African types of behavior are present among the Negroes of the United States, it is true, but on the basis of available data they are not of such a character as to localize provenience in the same way as can be done for Brazil, for Haiti, for Cuba, for Jamaica, for Suriname.

Especially first-generation Haitian Americans would be close to the culture of Benin. With this in mind, I decided to study the Catholic imagination in West Africa, focusing on Benin as my case study. This is how the idea for the study originated.

In April 2006, I benefited from a Fulbright award to lecture and conduct research on the Catholic imagination in Benin. On September 1, I arrived in

Cotonou, main city and economic capital. I left Benin on July 8, 2007 for two summer months in the United States.

During the preceding ten months—September to July—I was in the field, making contacts, attending celebrations and ceremonies, observing, conducting informational interviews. I traveled Benin north and south. Everything, everyone, every conversation, every celebration became a source of data. Even teaching served as research, since most students attending my host university, the *Institut Jean Paul II*, are from Benin or other countries of West Africa. The environment at the *Institut Jean Paul II*—a Catholic university—was conducive to this research on the Catholic imagination.

Not long after being in Benin, following several exploratory interviews with Catholics and adepts of the traditional Vodun religion, I came to realize in order to understand the Catholic imagination that it would be necessary to gain some understanding of the larger religious imagination in which it is embedded.

As reported to me in private communications with members of the hierarchy and lay Catholics, despite frowning from some religious leaders, popular Catholicism is mixed heavily with elements of traditional West African religion. This mixing may be considered similar to the religious mix found in Brazilian Candomblé where elements of Catholicism are wedded with traditional African religions (Parès, 2007). More than one scholar observed a similar mix in Haitian Christianity (Fils-Aimé, 2007; Desmangles, 1992; Métraux, 1958). Clearly, in Benin (as elsewhere) Catholicism is constructed from elements in the environment. In Benin, popular Catholicism is different from the American, the French, or any Catholicism in a non Beninese cultural setting.

While Catholicism is universal and its rituals, symbols and practice recognized worldwide, the specific cultural constructions and their importance will vary depending upon the socio-cultural context, more specifically the tools available in the immediate environment. Variations in these tools impact the Catholic imagination by shaping different Catholic imaginations. Variations reflected in rites and rituals, will also impact on the broader religious imagination which then acts back on the Catholic imagination. These ideas which await research are a more ambitious project than the issue of the nature of the Catholic imagination, its impact on acceptance of the other and on the religious practices of people of African descent addressed in this work. My Fulbright award was renewed for the 2007-2008 academic year. After two summer months in the United States, I returned to Benin to conduct the additional interviews.

Methodology

Following preliminary interviews and informal discussions with Catholics and Animists in Cotonou, a new interview guide was developed. For example, to understand the attitudes of interviewees toward interracial marriage, the original interview guide posed the question, "What would you do if your son or daughter married a white man?" While among social scientists in the United States the question would be an accepted measure of social/racial equality, preliminary interviews reveal it is not the case in Benin. Why? In Benin, being white means having money (perhaps, status also). Marrying white is sought after. As two informants put it, "We have to be honest with each other about this. It is an honor for a Beninese to marry someone white." Two university graduate students from Benin confirmed this view of marriage with whites. Thus the original question was modified to "how would you feel if your <u>son</u> married someone from another ethnic group?"

Notice a second modification to the question for obvious reasons—"ethnic" group rather than "racial." A question about sons marrying outside of their groups was also included. Benin is a patriarchal society. It is the son 'stayer'—not daughter—who transmits the family tradition to future generations. The absence of a son would disrupt the delicate balance inside a family. While in the earlier version of the interview guide, it was expected parents would react more strongly to their daughters marrying outside of the group, daughters leave home while sons stay behind. The question was rephrased to consider these local attitudes toward the out-marriage of sons and daughters.

Another way to capture acceptance is to inquire about marriage outside of one's religion. "How would you feel if your *son* married someone from another religion?" "How would you feel if your *daughter* married someone from another religion?" Finally, the interview guide also included a question about the respondent images of the United States and Europe—France especially. I reasoned this would broaden the research and provide important additional information about each religious group's thinking.

To further develop my understanding of the nature of Catholicism in Benin, I used comparison groups and broadened the interview population. In addition to Catholics, I spoke with Animists, Evangelicals, Celestials and Muslims. Cotonou, Ouidah, Abomey, Allada, Porto Novo (in the South) and Natitingou, Parakou (in the north), key cities in Benin, served as main sites for the interviews. The first respondents of these religious groups were recommended by key persons in their communities. Except for Cotonou, Catholic parishes from which the respondents originated were located in various sections of each city.

In Cotonou, two parishes offered a good choice of possible interviewees: *St. Michel* (in the *St. Michel* neighborhood) and *Bon Pasteur* (in the *Kajehoun* neighborhood*). Either parish would have been a good choice but most Catholic interviewees in Cotonou came primarily from *Bon Pasteur*. I selected *Bon Pasteur* because similar to *St Michel* in its demographic composition. *Bon Pasteur* is a large multiethnic, multi-class congregation that offers the diversity of respondent sought after. *Kadjehoun* is the neighborhood where resides President Dr. Boni Yayi and his wife Chantal. Madame Yayi runs a non-governmental agency also in *Kadjehoun*. *Kadjehoun* is adjacent to *Haie Vive*, the location of many embassies, and the upscale residence of diplomats and expatriates (usually known as *expats*). Nice restaurants and food markets reminders of the best European and American cater to these diplomats and other *yovos* (a word used for whites but sometimes foreigners or any race).

But *Bon Pasteur* is also close to *Gbégamey* and other non residential neighborhoods known as *bidonvilles*. These are popular neighborhoods with small businesses and many poorer homes sitting besides comparatively affluent ones. *Bon Pasteur* was also convenient geographically to my Catholic host university, the *Institut Jean Paul II*.

In Benin, there is no research *Institutional Review Board* (IRB). Before research begins, permission is sought from the *Ministère de l'Enseignement et de la Recherche Sociale*, a governmental agency. I submitted my request to do research through the American Cultural Center at the American Embassy in the form of a letter and shortly after was granted the official permission to proceed (see the index).

The field

In early December 2006, Dr. Alain Godonou, Director of *L'École du Patrimoine Africain* (EPA) and Dr. Gérard Tognimassou (Research Director) invited me to a conference in the historical city of Abomey. I developed many contacts among attendees. Most were Beninese journalists. It is here, at that conference, that I first became aware of an upcoming festival in the area to be held later in the month—a rare opportunity to collect data. Alain and Gérard introduced me to one of their assistants, Franck Ogou they described as interested, dynamic, and would be helpful to my research. I returned to Cotonou after this first meeting and a few weeks later, back again to Abomey to collect data, a chauffeur at the wheel and also accompanied by Franck.

Abomey.

My second visit to Abomey coincided with the festival and provided the opportunity to see, be seen by and meet more people. As part of the festival, authentic traditional religious ceremonies were performed in public for the local population. One of the Kings of Abomey—Agoli-Agbo was present. I did not see the popular King Béhanzin. The festival was an excellent opportunity to network. I met some key persons who later helped identify Catholic and Animist informants. Evangelicals and members of the Celestial Church of Christ were more difficult to locate. These contacts did not originate from the festival. The story of their meeting itself is interesting to tell.

Riding in my car, chauffeur at the wheel, I discovered an Evangelical Church with the name of the Pastor and his telephone number on the front wall. Standing outside of the car in front of the Church, I tried calling the Pastor. But contacting him via telephone was difficult given poor communication networks. Telephone contact made, the Pastor gave me his address and asked that I meet with him. Finding his home was another hurdle despite instructions that he himself offered. There are no names on the streets or numbers on houses. Road conditions made it worse. Eventually, his wife I met by chance in a nearby store where I stopped for directions, offered to join me to show the way to the house. The Pastor was at home as his wife had indicated. After greetings, I explained the project to him. He appeared interested and promised to coordinate the interviews to take place at the Evangelical Church on the following day. But in Benin, one should expect the unexpected. Things do not happen as planned.

Members of the Celestial Church of Christ were also difficult to reach. The hierarchy had gathered for a conference in Abomey. I met one of the *Supreme* of the Church as he was on his way to a Church conference. I caught his attention and gave him a brief description of my purpose in Abomey. He invited me to go along with him to the conference setting to speak about the project to some members of the Church. They too became interested, but before helping to organize the interviews, wanted me to seek permission directly from their President at his residence also in Abomey. I agreed.

Five or six members of the Celestial Church hierarchy, all men, dressed in their long white religious garb, entered the car and we drove to the house of the President. After hearing my description of the project, the President gave his approval. The next day, head covered and shoes removed, I visited the Celestial site in a secluded area and conducted several interviews. Here again, road conditions were difficult and as a result, I was not able to arrive on time for the afternoon interviews at the Evangelical Church. When I arrived at the Church, the potential respondents had come and left. No one was there. So, I returned to the Pastor's house, explained the reason for my late arrival. He was able to regroup some of the respondents (a very difficult task given poor communications, poor road conditions and unreliable transportation). The interviews took place at his residence that same afternoon.

In sum, access to Evangelicals and Celestials was difficult in Abomey. First it was necessary to identify key persons like the Evangelical pastor and the Supreme of the Celestial Church who would facilitate access to potential interviewees. Poor road conditions added to the difficulty of locating such persons, despite great help from my seventeen year old Mitsubishi Pajero and an experienced chauffeur who knew Abomey well. Eventually, Catholics, Evangelicals, Christian Celestials and Animists were identified. I conducted more than 25 interviews in Abomey.

Cotonou.

Cotonou was also difficult but in a different way. It is the economic capital and largest city where most people are busy making a living, earning their daily bread or looking to find this daily bread. Cotonou is similar to New York or Miami. It is also a city with the largest number of *zemidjans*—motorcycle taxis who will take you anywhere for a small cost. Zemidjans are a main form of transportation as taxis are rare, unreliable and expensive. *Zemidjans* identified by the bright yellow shirt of their driver (kekono) symbolize the bustling, risky life of Cotonou.

It is not easy for people to take time for an interview in Cotonou. And when an interview is scheduled, people may change their minds, forget, arrive late or for whatever reasons not show up. This "no show" is especially likely if the potential respondent knows that no *cadeau* (gift) will be offered. No matter how small, *faire un geste* or *cadeau* is always important and appreciated even if no service is rendered.

Despite these and other difficulties of the field, I had very productive interviews with at least 7 Catholics, 5 animists (10 informants from the previous year) and 5 Muslims. As in every city, questionnaires were distributed in addition to face-to-face interviews. Collecting these questionnaires was not a problem in the case of Catholics and Evangelicals, but difficult in case of Muslims and members of the Celestial Church of Christ.

Natitingou and Parakou.

Natitingou (*Nati*) is in the northern part of Benin in the Akatora region, not far from the Pendjari National Park where I saw a live lion in the wild for the first time. *Nati* was obviously different from Cotonou and Abomey. The city seemed dormant, less developed, with fewer people on the streets. The air is much cleaner and cooler than in the South. Life is slower than in the cities I visited or conducted research. The Muslim population was easier to reach than in Cotonou. But Animists were few, which may be explained by the strong presence of Islam in the North and Animism in the South.

Something interesting happened in Nati. In addition to the face-to-face interviews, my assistant and I also distributed questionnaires which 4 respondents took but refused to return because they demanded economic remuneration. This occurred even as these potential respondents were told ahead of time they would not receive money for their participation. Compared to the other cities, Natitingou was the least rewarding place to conduct interviews.

Parakou was more interesting than Natitingou even as some of the terrain continued to be rough. Most respondents had to be reached by way of motorcycle. I rode on the motorcycle of my assistant Gabin—a high school teacher, while one of Gabin's students ahead on his own motorcycle, guided us throughout the difficult roads. There were few members of the Celestial Church of Christ in this sample, but I was able to interview many Catholics, Muslims, Evangelicals and even Animists. Some of the most interesting interviews came from Parakou, a city with a strong French presence and much more developed than Natitingou.

Porto Novo, Allada, Ouidah.

Porto Novo is the administrative capital, home of the official site of the Celestial Church of Christ. The Celestial Church uses the term *Saint Siège* to refer to this site (emulating *Le Saint Siège* which is the Vatican. In fact they use a lot of

Catholic symbols and vocabulary). In Porto Novo, I interviewed a few Catholics, but most interviewees were Celestials and Evangelicals. An Islamic mosque is directly next to the Celestial Church but this should not be considered unusual given the coexistence of religions. I interviewed members of the Celestial Church at the *Saint Siège*.

Allada produced many insightful interviews. Clearly the topic was interesting to people who wanted to speak about their religion and thought the interviews offered them a unique chance to do so. But besides interviews, there are also personal reasons why Allada was interesting to me. It is the ancestral home of Toussaint L'Ouverture, liberator of Haiti. An oversize statue of General Toussaint L'Ouverture stands high in Allada for all to see. Below the statue, an encryption reads "General Toussaint L'Ouverture, digne fils d'Allada" with his dates of birth and death. Once a year, a public ceremony takes place here, attended by the King of Allada, the Queen, members of the Royal Court, as well as the delegation of the Haitian Embassy. These ceremonies are followed by a reception at the Royal Palace. In Allada, when people found out I grew up in Haiti, they seemed pleased. People know and admire Toussaint L'Ouverture. In Allada I spoke with many Catholics, some Animists and more Evangelicals than Celestials.

I also enjoyed Ouidah. The city has important historical and religious significance. I interviewed several Catholics but also some dignitaries of the Vodou religion, one I met by chance. I had been warned that he would be difficult to reach. But one early morning, while driving in front of his residence, I happen to see him outside and simply asked if I could have an interview. To my surprise, he said yes. This unexpected encounter made the interview even more valuable.

Wherever I went, I was received well. I was able to stay with nuns (in Natitingou and Abomey), at *Guy Riobé*, a Catholic hostel (in Parakou), at the home of the Church sacristan and his wife (in Allada). In Ouidah, I stayed at the rectory of *Basilique Notre Dame* and felt so honored when given the room reserved for bishops! It was actually a suite, with study, large bedroom with a double bed, and large bathroom. Père Jacynthe, a professor-priest at the *Institut Jean Paul II* to whom I related my surprise when offered these arrangements said to me jokingly "bien sûr, tu es une *évêque-este*."[15] Of course, he made up the word to provoke laughter.

Wherever I stayed, I felt welcome, found people interested in my research and willing to help identify respondents. I am grateful to all, and especially to the nuns at the *Foyer Ste Monique* in Abomey, at the religious residence in Nati, Ste Thérèse and *Guy Riobé* in Parakou, to Père Johnathan Capo-Chichi, Père Pardonou in Ouidah, Soeurs Catherine, Florence and Véronique in Abomey.

Whether Abomey, Natitingou, Parakou, Ouidah, Allada, Porto Novo, Cotonou, in every city, the field was the master directing data collection. Flexibility was key to success. I changed several aspects of my research while in the field. I modified questions, the number of persons to interview and how to select the respondents. The key was to find respondents who were as different as possible, except in their religious beliefs. Sometimes this model worked and sometimes it did not.

This research is not by the book. Replication would be difficult. No field is the same, and the same field may change with time.

Outline of chapters

This work is an attempt to understand the Beninese Catholic imagination and to discover its nature particularly in relation to diversity. What is the face of Catholicism in Benin? Is the Beninese Catholic imagination open to diversity and social justice? Another question of interest is this: Could the presence or absence of a Catholic imagination account for some of the differences observed between African diasporic cultures?

This first chapter explained the why and how of the study: to understand the Catholic imagination in its West African expression; to explain religious preferences observed in African diasporic groups, mainly African American and Haitian American. A second chapter queries the origin and nature of Catholicism in Benin before and after colonization. In a third chapter, the faithful speak about the impact of coexisting religions on their lives. This chapter also delves into the meaning of inculturation. A fourth chapter centers on power in the extended family, the part it plays in negotiating social order, and the outcome of negotiations from double belonging (syncretism) to inculturation. Using the ethnogenesis perspective in combination with negotiated order (better yet, border) the fifth chapter addresses the question: "What can be learned about the Catholic imagination, its relation to acceptance (religious and ethnic) and its contributions to difference between African diasporic cultures?

Chapter Two
Why West Africa?

A curious feature of West Africa is the religious toler-
ance, especially in the coastal area, where members of
different religions live together in such harmony that
they may join in one another's festivals. . . .[I]t is not
uncommon to find Christian, Muslim and Animist in
the same family (Parrinder, 1959: 134).

From Melville Herskovits we learn the importance of going to the source to understand the origin of cultures, including the cultures of the African diaspora. As
Herskovits (Herskovits, 1933: 247) puts it,

> A knowledge of the provenience of the Negroes of the New World is
> basic to the study of New World Negro cultures, since to comprehend
> the cultural equipment with which these people entered upon their lives
> in the western hemisphere is essential in any successful attempt to util-
> ize the materials gained from investigations of their present-day life for
> an analysis of the processes of cultural change and of the results of cul-
> ture-contact.

Of course, Herskovits' language distances him from African cultures, especially
when he refers to 'the Negroes of the New World' and 'these people.' But it was
the language of the time. Moreover, my interest is not so much the language of
Herskovits as his idea that returning to the motherland can shed light on diasporic cultures.

In the preceding chapter, I shared one of my goals in this work: to explain
the religious preferences of Haitian- and African-Americans. Turning to Africa,
the source was an important first step. "Africanisms are the residue, vestige, or
cultural elements born in Africa, thus the presence of Africanisms in diasporic
cultures of the Caribbean and other regions in the Western Hemisphere serve as

evidence of African origin." Herskovits is convinced it is possible to trace the ancestry of diasporic populations not only to the African continent but also to specific regions in Africa. "Thus we see that the Africanisms in the Negro cultures of South America and the islands of the Caribbean, not only point to specific regions in Africa, but that the evidence supports the hypothesis of provenience . . ." (Herskovits, 1933: 259-260). To Herskovits' statement could be added that the absence or near absence of Africanisms in a population is evidence of post-slavery experience.

Importance of Benin

When returning to the African source, Benin specifically is important to consider. The former Dahomey holds special place in this "historical provenience." In a review of historian Robin Law's book that author Lovejoy (1994: 328) thought the "best historical study of an African religion in the scholarly literature," Lovejoy (1991: 327) writes:

> Benin was one of the most important sources of slaves for the Americas, and perhaps for a few decades in the early eighteenth century, the ports of the Slave Coast exported more slaves than any other comparable stretch of the African shore. Europeans gave this region its name for a good reason. Dahomey, Allada, and Whydah figure prominently in the history of the slave trade.

Herskovits (1933: 259) agrees, for he too recognizes the historical "evidence points to Dahomey as the principal source of its Negro culture . . . . [although t]here is little in the literature concerning the non-religious aspects of life." More recent works also acknowledge the diasporic connections with Dahomey (see also Herskovits, 1939).

Whatever segment or aspect of the diaspora is being considered—whether Jamaican, Jamaican American, Haitian, Haitian American, African American, or other—explanation begins with West Africa. Even more relevant is this historical provenience to a study of religion for "[r]eligion is one of the most important influences in human life, and it is as strong in West Africa as anywhere" (Parrinder, 1960: 38). In Benin, I attempted to interview atheists—persons who did not believe in a higher being. I found none. This is not to say they do not exist. They probably do. But if so they are rare and, given the popularity of religion, would be more difficult to identify than believers. In a society where religion is so important, so visible, so expected of each member, social desirability would likely drive "deviant non believers" underground. These "irreligious marginals" would be society's undesirables. While France and Europe in general are said more and more secularized,[16] religion is spreading so quickly in Africa some scholars even speak of the possibility of a "reverse evangelization." A reversal means Africans are and/or will be, Christianizing the American and European continents. In the United States, the popularity of African priests whose numbers are increasing in Catholic parishes provides some evidence of this trend in reverse evangelization.

Because it is recognized as one original source of diasporic cultures, a return to West Africa and the former Dahomey can shed light on people of the diaspora and on differences among them, including in the religious sphere. To understand diasporic cultures and their religious behaviors, it is necessary to return to the motherland West Africa.

Birthplace of diasporic cultures.

Herskovits (1933: 260) links to West African culture some religious behaviors displayed by African Americans.

> [I]t is possible to see expressions of religious ritual that would not be out of place in West African tribal villages. One witnesses spirit possession, thought by the 'Holy Ghost,' dancing with the identical steps and the same motor behavior that characterizes the worship of aboriginal African gods; singing that derives, in manner if not in actual form, directly from Africa.

But Herskovits also noted not all diasporic cultures are the same. There are differences between them. For example, though elements of West African culture are evident in African American religious behaviors, these elements are far from being as distinctive and as recognizable as those found in other African diasporic cultures. Not all diasporic cultures exhibit the same levels or "types of [religious] behavior."

> Generalized West African types of behavior are present among the Negroes of the United States, it is true, but on the basis of available data they are not of such a character as to localize provenience in the same way as can be done for Brazil, for Haiti, for Cuba, for Jamaica, for Suriname (Herskovits, 1933: 262).

Herskovits' statement is important for this research. It suggests cultural (including religious) differences between native-born African Americans and first generation Haitian Americans may be rooted in variations of types and levels of cultural retention. Differences among Haitian Americans, African Americans and other diasporic groups may be reflected also in the less researched culinary arts and music, as well as other more important areas as language (including body language) and religion.

Physically the people of Benin look Haitian. One may be correct in asking 'what is the Haitian look?' While this statement about "looks" may not "sound sociological" because some would argue it cannot be measured, I will say it anyway. I say this because I felt—yes, felt—a real physical connection with the people of Benin. Often I thought I knew someone who so reminded me of a Haitian friend, old acquaintance or sometimes even member of my family. One Beninese colleague at my host University so resembled my own father, I had to share that observation. My father who passed away many years ago had never been to Africa. Yet the resemblance is striking. After four decades in the United States I do not recall ever having had that experience. There are many aspects of society that sociologists attempt to measure, but are not actually measurable. I suggest this as one of them and repeat without objective measurement that the people of Benin "look Haitian."

On culinary arts, what is known as the Haitian national dish *poi colé ak diri* (red beans and rice) is popular in Benin. It is even sold already prepared at the open market. While a similar dish called "rice and beans" may be found in Louisiana that version is different from the Haitian in spice and presentation. Staying with the example of foods, I have always thought specifically Haitian such delicacies as *accrats* prepared in Haiti and the kitchens of Haitian Americans. But *accrats* are also prepared in Benin with outcome close to the Haitian even as the name and some ingredients vary. In Benin, there is also an equivalent to the Haitian *akassan* (corn based breakfast cereal) and a dish similar to the famous Haitian staple *maïs moulu ak poi*. Though presented differently, the latter tastes much like the delicious Beninese *amiyo*.[17] Researching African American culinary arts to see if there are dishes equivalent to the ones previously mentioned and others would make an interesting and important diasporic project.

Driving or walking down the streets of Cotonou, one hears popular West African music whose rhythm is a striking reminder of the Haitian. On a few occasions when I turned to Golfe, ORTB (Office de Radiodiffusion du Bénin) or other television channels for a taste of traditional music, dance and colorful costumes I was struck by their similarities to folkloric songs of Haiti, though as in the case of physical resemblance not able to point specifically to what are these similarities. It is a certain familiarity with the sounds, steps, colors, combination of colors, and a general sense that Benin, Haiti and their peoples are closely related. African American music sometimes heard in Benin is different from the Haitian and Beninese. Dance steps are also reminders of what might be observed in Haiti during traditional ceremonies, or public performances of folklore.

When Beninese people speak or sing in the *fon-gbe* dialect (most commonly spoken in the southern region), I am reminded of Haitian Creole. Clearly, words in *fon-gbe* are different from Haitian Creole and except for everyday greetings, I do not know what is being said. Yet the voice, intonation, inflexion, words spoken, songs sung, all are reminders of Haitian ways of speaking, intonating, inflexing, and singing. In early email communications from Benin, I mentioned repeatedly how much I felt as if I were in Haiti.

Religious similarities with Haiti are also obvious. Some West African Vodou divinities have equivalents in Haitian Vodou (see Fils-Aimé, 2006). Catholic Haitian American Midwesterners interviewed in the early 2000 were aware of this long presence of Vodou in Haitian culture. However, in general, African American respondents seemed to distance themselves from Vodou. In these same interviews, they did not dwell on the topic.

Religious differences are salient. To understand religious (or other important) differences among peoples of the African diaspora it is necessary to return
to West African sources to see how these might have originated and their consequence for diasporic cultures. Of course, a return to the source is an especially
difficult task because having to rely primarily on the writings of European missionaries. The missionary perspective on African culture is not impartial. Early
missionaries were not African. Even the best intentioned saw Africa through
European eyes, thus used a standard for judgment that was European or *yovo*—
not West African. The consequences of returning to and learning uncritically
from these *yovo* sources are obvious. Little need is there to spell them out.

Many authors recognize the partiality in European perception in their writings about Africans. Take for example Christine Hardung's work in the north of
Benin (Eckert and Jones, 2002: 11).

> Having established that the answers given by colonial officials to question-
> naires in the first decade of the twentieth century are not very helpful when
> looking at slaves' living conditions, [Hardung] turns to the oral narratives of
> old people who were formerly slaves. While recognizing the methodological
> problems involved in relying upon the recollections of 'those who would rather
> forget', she shows how in such circumstances body language can itself consti-
> tute a form of memory. Her conclusion—on the need to take present-day social
> realities into account when drawing upon remembered histories of life in the
> colonial period—is of relevance to all kinds of work on everyday life.

Hardung recognized the problems associated with historical research, the perceptions of colonizers doing research and the need to speak directly to local people when observing and writing about everyday African life even though these
recollections are often muddled, fluid and reconstructed. Recollections would
come closer to real everyday life. More importantly, it would be the very historical perceptions of the people. It is therefore imperative to lay critical eyes on
documents provided by foreign missionaries.

Earlier, this work highlighted what seem to be retentions in one diasporic
culture—Haitian. But cultural "retention" means only parts of the original cultures—not all of it—survived. Foreign intrusion has its impact on physical appearance, culinary arts, music, language, everyday living, being and believing.
But another similarity Haiti shares with Benin is colonization by the French.
Haiti earned her independence from the French in January 1804; Benin, in 1960.
These additional similarities in the historico-cultural experience of colonization
infuse the Haitian diasporic and original cultures, again keeping these two populations culturally close. Thus as additional source of closeness with Benin, colonization by the French helps to assess further those similarities between Benin
and Haiti and cultural differences between Haitian Americans and African
Americans. African American culture was shaped by English American Protestantism and Protestant values.

Of course, it would be interesting to study the difference between African
Americans of Louisiana where French Catholic influence has been strong and

native African Americans in regions where historically Protestantism has pre-
vailed, and influenced ways of thinking, living, being and believing. African
Americans in Louisiana would have much more in common with Haitian
Americans, including in the religious sphere. It seems also that Louisiana Afri-
can Americans would be closer than other African Americans to the Beninese.
Regional differences are important.

Pre and post Catholicism

It is back to the source. This section peruses Benin before colonization, but, as
already mentioned, recognizes the potential for bias in the literature, including
current writings by Beninese authors.

Benin is the new name for the old Dahomey. Dahomey is the name for an
ancient kingdom (Triaca, 1997: 27). The name Dahomey marks a time when the
population was guided by ancestral norms (Triaca, 1997: 28). Before Europeans
arrived, Benin had an oral tradition. Documents were kept in memory. Europeans brought the written tradition with them. According this oral tradition, around
the 12th or 13th century, the southwest region of the country was inhabited by the
Adja people. Approximately 2000 years ago, the Adja migrated from Ile-Ife, the
Nigerian city that people in the south of Benin consider their religious capital.
This migration left Tado, on the western "rive" of the Mono River, today a
Togolese territory. This town became the cradle of the population of south Be-
nin (Triaca, 1997: 30).

What is Vodoun? Vodoun are "invisible powers with the possibility to intervene at anytime on men." These powers or divinities "represent . . . the link
between the visible and the invisible, between man and divine nature, living and
the dead, the temporal and the surnatural. . . . Ancestors who have become divinities control nature as well as human activities including "hunting, work,
metals."

> 'Le pouvoir . . . de l'ancêtre vodun aurait la faculté après sa mort, de se
> transmettre momentanément à un de ses descendants au cours d'une transe de
> possession.' Ainsi, les hommes peuvent directement communiquer avec leur
> divinité, le monde de l'au-delà est ainsi proche (Badufle, 1999: 98).

> [The power of the Vodun ancestor would have the ability, after death, to trans-
> mit itself momentarily to one of his descendants during a trance. So men can
> directly communicate with their divinity, the world beyond is thus near].

Vodun was the original religion of Benin. In the 12th century, Catholicism was
introduced, first by the Capuchins priests who failed in their attempt to evangelize the kingdom of Allada. In the 19th century Protestants led a movement of
Christian evangelization. These Protestants were followed by Catholic missionaries who in 1861, settled in Ouidah with priests Borghero and Fernandez.
Around 1851, Protestants settled in Porto-Novo (Badufle,1999: 53).

Catholics had a difficult time at the very beginning. But, between years 1905 and 1955 Catholicism bloomed guided by Mgr Steinmetz (1906-1934), supported by the colonial system and the work of the Révérend Père Aupiais in education.

> A partir des années 1890, le Dahomey devient véritablement propice à l'action des missionnaires catholiques qui sont largement soutenus par l'appareil colonial devenu français. L'arrivée en 1903, de Mgs. R. P. Aupiais marquera d'ailleurs l'essor scolaire au Dahomey (Badufle, 1999: 53; 54).

> [Beginning with the years 1890, Dahomey becomes really precious to the actions of Catholic missionaries largely supported by the colonial apparatus turned French. The arrival in 1903 of Mgr. R. P. Aupiais marks the educational spring forward of Dahomey.]

So, the beginning of Catholicism in Benin corresponds with the successful educational advancements under Père Aupiais. Here too began the development of Catholic churches. Interestingly, "the parents of founders were adepts of Vodun or sometimes pagans (without precise religion), except for the mother parish of Djerege, where the founder, a European, had Catholic parents" (Badufle, 1999: 56). The founders of Catholic churches had a mixed set of religious affiliations.

> Three were Vodun before converting to Catholicism, three declared having always been Catholic (they were baptized as infants, whereas 2 of them, had parents who were not Catholic), finally, one of the founders is a former Boda-Owa (Protestant). The creation of churches was done under the impulsion of missions, except for churches established in 1997 whose founders converted either by personal will for one, or by revelation after a trip to the Ivory Coast for the other (Badufle, 1999: 56).

These founders recorded observations and experiences. But Benin had and still has an oral culture. Words were important then and they are important now. Words have power. Words are sacred. Yet Benin's early history was written, thus shaped by a European point of view. Europeans used the power of their ethnocentric pen. And though the interpretations of Beninese historians may be different and more grounded in local culture, they too look at the past using as their primary sources these writings of Europeans. For that reason, the writings of West African historical writers must be taken critically as well.

Idowu (1973: 83) writes, "One of the great obstacles in the way of the study of African traditional religion is, of course, the lack of written records by Africans of their ancient past. All that we have from indigenous African are the oral traditions." Though not free of errors, the least ethnocentric works with an insider interpretation are likely those of African authors.

Beninese historian A. Felix Iroko identifies two major factors that influenced *La Côte des Esclaves* (the Slave Coast): Vodun and the slave trade. It is in the religious context of Vodun that the slave trade began (Iroko, 2003: 183).

While Iroko places equal responsibility on Africans and Europeans for the trade (in exchange for their brothers and sisters, Africans received violins, mirrors, and other such objects), he blames Christian Europe for an image of itself as advanced that helped target "less advanced" others and bring them light and civilization (Iroko, 2003: 185).

Africans fell for the idea that the Europeans had greater knowledge and could lead them to a better tomorrow. Europeans were thought more religious because they gave the Africans reasons to think they, the Europeans, were more religious. According to historian Alphonse Quénum, ships that transported the enslaved to the New World had Christian names such as "Santa Catalina à Santissimo Sarameneto e Nossa Senhora, Santa Cruz, Jesus, Grâce de Dieu, Rosario et Nuestra Senora de la Esperanza (Quénum, 1970: 301).

As models of goodness, the Europeans could be trusted—so the Africans thought. It has been suggested that if the Africans who sold their brothers to the Europeans knew what their brother's and sister's fate would be, that the trade would not have taken place, at least on such a large scale. But, of course, this remains speculation.

The European presentation-of-good-self did not prevent traditional religion. Another factor that helped to retain the practice of Vodou tradition among the enslaved is this: during the slave trade there was no systematic effort to evangelize the African continent (Quénum 1970: 302). From the very beginning, Animism and more specifically Vodun were strong religious beliefs that continued to be practiced among the enslaved. Vodou was the traditional religion. It was the popular religion—the religion of the people—which shaped that popular and cultural imagination. During that time, ancestor worship was widespread (see for example Addisson, 1924; Law, 1991; Lovejoy, 1994). James Thayer Addison, an Episcopalian missionary writes, the

> Evidence for the existence of ancestor worship among the *uncivilized 18* peoples of Africa is varied and abundant. . . . The devotion to ancestors in Dahomey, however, is not limited to the kings alone, for members of the upper classes are accustomed to place in their houses the skulls of those who have been dead for more than a few years and to appeal to them for advice and assistance (Thayer Addison, 1924: 156;157).

Note, in this statement, the use of "uncivilized," a reflection of the perception among missionaries that ancestor worship was a form of savagery, and the peoples of West Africa (Dahomey, in particular) needed to be "civilized."

Animism and ancestor worship were the religious situation prior to and even after the arrival of Europeans. But ancestor worship is still prevalent today in contemporary West Africa. Inside houses in some areas of Benin, altars for the worship of ancestors may still be found. Familial ceremonies are common. Here, I share a personal experience.

A friend invited me to a village near the city of Ouidah during the Christmas season to visit her aunt. A relative had recently passed away and plans, were being made for the funeral. Plans included widening the road that led to the house of the deceased (quite an expensive project). The deceased was to be buried inside the house, what used to be her bedroom directly in front of the bed. The area to be dug for the burial had been marked. In Benin, the dead are not dead but continue to be part of the family.

When we arrived at the residence, and after formal greetings, which included offering us water and in this case *sodabe* (a hard alcohol called *clairin* in Haiti) this aunt took us immediately to a separate small dwelling which had a low narrow entrance door, and was located in the backyard. We had to bend in order to get inside this dwelling. As for entrance in any sacred place, removing our shoes was a precondition.

Once we were inside with our shoes off, Aunt Vera (not her real name) accompanied us to an area that had a hole in the ground and inside and around this hole, several objects. I could not tell with a casual look how deep was the hole nor could I see clearly what these objects were or how many.

I stood behind my friend at some distance from the center stage. As she put money in the hole, her aunt who remained closer to and bent over it began a prayer in *fon-gbe*. Though I could not understand the words being pronounced or what exactly was being said, I could tell the prayer was intense based upon the vocal force that accompanied each word. I also believed, based upon the context, the prayer was being offered to ancestors for my friend and for me, to protect us from harm. My friend suggested that, out of respect, I too make a small donation. I moved toward the hole and placed this donation (10,000 cfa— a little over 20 U.S.dollars—next to the unidentified objects.

This telling event suggests even in a West African neo colonial era, tradition still prevails and ancestor worship is alive. My friend, a medical professional also a fervent Catholic who attends daily Mass, is close to the Catholic hierarchy.

On our way back home to Cotonou, I shared with her my fear that donating money, however small the amount, was participation which would be unethical given my personal beliefs, and the fact that as a researcher, I was not engaging in participant observation—at least in this particular case. She reassured me what I had seen and experienced had nothing to do with Vodou. Aunt Vera is a practicing Catholic who was simply honoring the long tradition of showing respect for, seeking advice and favors from, ancestors. Aunt Vera's prayers, my money gesture and my friend's, were only signs of respect.

Among questions raised by the event are the following: Where does tradition (which includes religion) end? Where does modernity (which includes Christianity) begin? How far goes negotiation between past and present? It would be interesting to ponder on the similarities between this show of respect to ancestors in the Beninese context, and the Western tradition of visiting (and placing flowers on) graves? Isn't this just a different form of showing respect for ancestors long ago and more recent ones?

Habits of tolerance: negotiating every day

It has been suggested that religious tolerance has long prevailed in West Africa.

> A curious feature of West Africa is the religious tolerance, especially in the coastal area, where members of different religions live together in such harmony that they may join in one another's festivals. . . . Among the Yoruba it is not uncommon to find Christian, Muslim and Animist in the same family (Parrinder, 1959: 134).

Tolerance is still the case today. In the previous example, my friend medical professional and self-identified fervent Catholic, showed much respect for tradition—the family tradition—and found that tradition compatible with her practice of Catholicism. It is the same with Aunt Vera, identified by her niece as good Catholic. Aunt Vera seemed not to experience conflict between her practice of local traditions on the one hand and, on the other, her practice of Catholicism.

Tolerance of religious beliefs is also evident at the national level, where special days are set aside to celebrate Islam, celebrate Vodou, and celebrate Christianity. When it comes to feast days no religious group is favored. An example of tolerance often cited in the literature and described by respondents are the history and location of the *Basilique Immaculée Conception*. The impressive grayish Church structure stands tall and strong in the city of Ouidah. Many official Catholic ceremonies take place here including more recently, one of many tributes to the life of Bernardin Cardinal Gantin before inhumation at Ouidah's *St. Gall*'s seminary. The Basilica is located directly across *Le Temple des Pythons*, a Vodou temple. When one is inside the Church facing out, it is not possible to miss the sign that marks the temple. This suggests, when the priest is saying Mass facing his congregation, he too is privileged to that same view of the temple (though the sight may be too familiar to be noticed at all). Moreover, though this may come as a shock to Catholics of other nations, adepts of Vodou helped in the construction of the Basilica. In Benin, this sort of religious cooperation is business as usual. Perhaps one of many reasons for this solidarity is the people's knowledge that the mother of the highly respected (now deceased) Monseigneur Isidore de Souza was a *vodounsi*.

Rather than treating the history of solidarity around the construction of the Basilica as unique, one informant links this example of multicultural tolerance to traditional culture and religion: "There are many divinities in the pantheon Vodun and West Africans are used to each other worshiping one or the other divinity. There is religious interaction. They accept the beliefs of the other." From this viewpoint, acceptance of the other is anchored in the traditional religious system, the culture and popular imagination. Internal religious diversity is externalized and extended to other areas of life. There is a religious "predisposition" to cultural and religious diversity and solidarity. One consequence is the problem of religious demographics.

Tolerance and demography.

In Benin it appears that religious faiths coexist. But while tolerance seems to prevail and be anchored in traditional religion, "[t]here are very few census returns available to give an indication of religious affiliations, and those few that exist are not above suspicion" (Parrinder, 1960: 38). This statement nearing five decades still applies. Today, demographic statistics are not consistent. The difficulty of obtaining reliable numbers on religious affiliations is not only due to problems of data collection in a developing society but also to this coexistence of faiths, Vodou-infused traditions and Christian modernity side-by-side in a neocolonialist society.

The Archdiocese of Cotonou does keep reliable statistics on the number of churches, parishioners (foreigners and native) the total number of Catholics, other Christians, non-Christians (Animists, Muslims), numbers of baptisms, first communions, confirmations, and marriages, in the city of Cotonou. For obvious reasons, statistics are not available for villages. The statistics collected by the Archdiocese of Cotonou are likely more accurate than the governmental but here too a large margin of error must be taken into account.[19]

Despite the general lack of accurate statistics however, we know generally that in various parts of West Africa, some religious faiths are more popular than others. For example, "There are many areas of West Africa where Islam is dominant, but there are others where it is still less influential than Animism or Christianity, Eastern Nigeria, southern Dahomey and Togo, the south of Ghana and the southern Ivory Coast still have few Muslims" (Parrinder, 1959: 135). This variation in religious influence is also accurate for Benin where Islam is strong in the northern region with Catholicism and Vodou strong in the south. A researcher interested for example in an interview study of Islam (unless, of course, the topic is perceptions) would turn north for information, whereas information about Catholicism, Vodou, and the Celestial Church of Christ (again, not dealing with perceptions) is best sought in the southern region—especially along the coast where adepts of these faiths are more numerous. Since this study tried to understand the nature of Catholicism in Benin, though Catholics and others faiths are also interviewed in the north, most data on Catholics were collected in the central and southern regions where Catholics are more populous.

Tolerance and Religious Beliefs in Everyday Life

The tendency towards tolerance leads us to ask what the people believe. Earlier, I argued in Benin, that there is a tendency to religious and cultural diversity, to solidarity and tolerance. However, there could also be a common belief linking these religious faiths. There could be a shared belief in a higher Being whether God, *Mawu*, *Allah*, or some of the many other appellations for this Being. I looked for atheists to interview, people who did not believe in a higher being, but had difficulty finding them. Most people believe in something bigger than themselves. So comes the puzzling question: Was the belief in that "Something Bigger" introduced by European missionaries? Or, since so widespread, could it possibly be rooted in traditional religion? Did it precede Europeans?

One observer of the African scene writes "All these polytheists believe in a Supreme Being, chief and creator called by a variety of names: . . . Mawu . . ." (Parrinder, 1960: 38). Early authors this observer writes, including the celebrated Pierre Verger, were wrong in thinking that the idea of God came to Africa from Europe:

> The older European writers used to think that the idea of God must have been introduced from Europe, and this has been suggested again by Pierre Verger in his book *Notes sur le Culte des Orisa et Vodun* (Dakar 1957). Verger says that some Yoruba told him that Olorun was the God of the Christians, and others that Olodumare was the Muslim God, while the local village god was generally supreme; in any case, he concludes, 'the eyes of men in their ceremonies are turned not towards the sky but towards the earth. The nourishing earth, the earth which contains the bodies of the ancestors' (Parrinder, 1960: 38, 39).

According to this author, for Pierre Verger and other European writers, the Supreme Being is located above, in the sky, and ancestors are below, in the earth. To worship ancestors is to stay close to the profane, material world, whereas eyes turned to the sky and above, mean looking in the direction of the Supreme God, the spiritual and sacred.

Continues Parrinder:

> On the other hand Dr. E. B. Idowu in his thesis on the Yoruba idea of God says that belief in Olodumare as supreme is ancient and pre-European. And Harry Sawyer of Sierra Leone affirms that 'in the rituals of worship and sacrifice, God is never altogether left out. In the case of rites involving the dead ancestors, one gets the impression that their aid is invoked to secure the blessings of God particularly in times of crisis' (Parrinder, 1960: 39).

The point being made is this: Ancestor worship which is prevalent in the tradition and religion does not necessarily eliminate beliefs in the nonmaterial world, the idea of the sacred. There are comments in the interviews to support traditional beliefs in a Supreme Being.

The Daah and higher dignitaries of traditional religion I interviewed talk about God as Supreme Being above all men, above divinities, thus above lesser gods. Traditional priests consider these divinities or gods intermediaries to the Supreme Being so far above men that He can only be reached through their intercessions. This thinking could be referred to as the Vodou imagination, an imagination that sees the invisible in the visible. The Supreme Being is materialized through lesser but visible beings. It is interesting that the Catholic imagination has been defined as "seeing the invisible in the visible" (see chapter 1).

Here, I return to the example of Aunt Vera who while believing in a Supreme Being found it necessary to seek the intercessions of her ancestors.

Thus there seems a certain level of confusion in the interpretations of European writers who appear not to have understood traditional culture and the complexity involved in everyday West African religious practices. The same confusion is evident in interviews with Evangelicals, several of whom thought traditionalists not guided by their beliefs in a Supreme Being but rather by their beliefs in something closer to a material world. Yet, the Animist presentation of self is very different. While ancestors of the old past and the ones more recent influence everyday life, Vodou is presented by adepts first and foremost as belief in a Supreme Being but also in powerful intermediary divinities that are closer to this Being and can intervene in everyday life. They are assistants to the Supreme Being.

About everyday religious life.

This work is about everyday life. But what is so important about everyday life?

> Does it make sense to introduce this category into the study of colonial Africa? [even contemporary Africa]. Whilst the quotidianist perspective does not necessarily yield radically new insights into Africa's colonial history . . . such a perspective does require a shift of emphasis on the part of Africanist historians. First, it was primarily the subtle changes in everyday life that determined the manner in which modern Africa emerged; secondly, this perspective obliges us to transcend the dichotomy between colonizers and the colonized, viewing them rather as part of the same analytical field; and thirdly, writing the history of everyday life requires us to think in open systems, in which historians deal with a multitude of competing versions of history. This polyphony can be welcomed: everyday-life history shows that it is possible to live with contradictions without falling into the arbitrariness of postmodernism (Eckert and Jones, 2002: 13).

There are more reasons why a focus on everyday life is important. It allows a more accurate view of the people, their thinking and their practices—religious, or other. In everyday life, people can speak for themselves about their present, about their past, without their words being filtered through often inaccurate translations or foreign interpretations.

This work is about popular West African Catholicism in everyday life. Everyday religion is popular religion practiced everyday. Religious behaviors, even rituals are a part of this every day life for, what to outsiders may seem repeated or patterned behaviors are also infused with a refreshing spontaneity characteristic of the moment and every day. We know from Eckert and Jones (2002: 6),

> as a marker of special occasions in the life of individuals and communities, ritual is often defined in opposition to the everyday. On the other hand, outsiders

and visitors notice everyday rituals such as ways of eating or forms of greeting in the life of every society, which the locals fail to perceive as rituals at all.

Moreover, "While the concept of 'everyday life' has provoked a widely recognized and often highly controversial debate in European and American history, it has hitherto been more or less neglected in the context of African history" (Eckert and Jones, 2002: 6). The everyday life perspective has also been neglected in religious studies (see Ammerman, 2006).

This work about everyday life also includes rituals. It is about what real people do (observation), what they say they do (interviews), and what they report observing other people do in every day religious life (interviews). The idea and possibility of religious mixing triggered many interesting discussions of everyday life in interviews. Though they do not use these exact terms, syncretism, double or multiple religious belonging, inculturation among Catholics and others are themes often raised and linked to the past by respondents. Religious mixing or double religious belonging in everyday life offers another convenient approach to studying popular Catholicism, acceptance of the other, and difference between diasporic cultures.

Conclusion

West Africa, birthplace of diasporic cultures provides an important historical context for the study of the Catholic imagination in everyday life and the behaviors and preferences of Africa's diasporic cultures. Vodun was the original religion. Missionary education helped spread Catholicism and what today appear various syncretic religions. Catholicism in Benin may be envisioned as the outcome of historical negotiations between missionaries (guardian of Catholic borders) and the adepts of traditional religion (guardian of Vodun borders).

Chapter three
Presentation of Sacramental Self

> Inculturation . . . is not traditional
> religion. It is the culture; what is good in the culture
> and gives an answer . . . that is, where the baptized . . .
> can find himself, that's all. That is really to find him-
> self and to say that, "that is mine."
> Inculturation is a good thing.

How does the Catholic imagination express itself in Benin? How is Catholicism lived? One characteristic of Beninese popular Catholicism is the presence of traditional elements as in the story of Aunt Vera. I begin this chapter with additional examples some of them personal to deepen insights into this Catholic imagination. Later, the respondents speak for themselves.

For several months, I live in a three-story rented house located in the Patte d'Oie neighborhood of Cotonou, between my host university the *Institut Jean Paul II* (John Paul II Institute) and the *Collège des Prêtres* (College of Priests) a boarding house for clergy from West Africa studying in Benin. The house, known as *La Thérésienne*, in fact the entire block belongs to the Archdiocese of Cotonou. On the same side of the street stand other buildings also property of the Archdiocese: a 4-story rental apartment dwelling that helps finance the Institut; a Catholic secondary school *Collège Père Aupiais*; a Catholic hostel *Le Chant d'Oiseau* which welcomes researchers from all over the world; and a little further away, the Archdiocese, official residence of Monsignor Marcel Honorat Léon Agboton, Archbishop of Cotonou. *Bon Pasteur*, a popular multi-class, multi-ethnic parish stands across the main street, not far from this neighborhood.

Every day Mass is celebrated at the Archdiocese, the hostel, the secondary school, the Collège des Prêtres, the Institut and Bon Pasteur. The frequency of Mass would seem startling in comparison to the United States where the current reality is a shortage of religious vocations and in many parishes, daily Mass has become something of the past.

Mass celebration at the Chapel of the Institute is not close enough to hear the daily prayers or music from my house. Only on special occasions do I hear these, when a crowd in attendance is moved to the large 500+ capacity auditorium. But the Collège of Priests is close enough for the sounds of songs in French, Fong-be, sometimes Mina, to escape the intimacy of the Chapel, penetrate the interior of the house and other nearby spaces—sacred and not-so-sacred. Songs in French are usually traditional. I heard them when growing up in Haiti and other Catholic contexts.

At the end of Mass, songs in Fon-gbe enliven the faithful. Clapping sounds, vocal sounds, tapping over the mouth, *tam-tams* and other West African instruments pierce with force the walls of the Chapel. Usually, closing songs are about Mary, an icon constantly venerated in Benin. The popularity of Mary is another difference with the United States where she is remembered specifically during the months of May and October, the Feast of the Assumption on August 15, the Feast of Immaculate Conception on December 8, and the Feast of Mary Mother of God on January 1. For the most part, Mary and the rosary have faded or simply become memory, though this may not apply to ethnic parishes (especially Mexican American)

I hear sounds of *tam tams* (musical instruments) escaping the Chapel. I hear the faithful speak with their bodies and voices. Sometimes I hear them laugh. Sometimes I see dancing. I see an altar boy, left hand on his chest, right hand holding a gold container of incense, moving it back, forth, around in repeated motions. I imagine the incense rising through the air. I imagine its spiritually enhancing effects on the faithful. Cheek against the window, I recall my own experience participating in these religious celebrations.

Whether at the Collège des Prêtres, Père Aupiais, Chant d'Oiseau, or Bon Pasteur, religious celebrations are a mix of tradition and modernity—French and Fon-gbe, sometimes Mina or occasionally Latin. Bon Pasteur lacks intimacy because so vast, but it also offers a broad array of sacramentals in large sizes—big statues, big stations of the cross, numerous flames dancing on top of candles, in other words more and bigger "paraphernalia"[20] that may have a wide range of effects on the faithful. At Bon Pasteur, altar boys (not girls as may often be seen in the United States) enter the Church in procession, followed by deacons ahead of the celebrant. They wear bright yellow robes and facing the altar, move forward to the beat of choir music. Behind this altar for all to see is a wall painted yellow on which rests the giant cross with a dark bronzed figure representing Christ. A tata sumba-shaped repository seats at the left of the altar and to the right are a few chairs for celebrant and deacon, similar in shape to those used by kings. There is a traditional "pagne" fabric covering the table. Sometimes, the chasuble of the celebrant carries a symbol of Marie or a map of Africa.

At Bon Pasteur (and other churches similar or almost similar in size like St. Michel or Père Aupiais) one observes excitement in the congregation particularly during a second collection called "Action de Grace" [thanks giving] when instruments and voices gain in rhythm, spreading within the Church an epidemic of generosity. And in a society that suffers from economic poverty, people are generous indeed, judging from the number of old and young, most in traditional clothing but some in western outfits, who get up from their seats, move to various locations inside the Church where baskets await their gifts of money. Sometimes they walk to the beat of music.

Throughout Mass, participation and collective effervescence unite the faithful. Colors, languages, songs, are a mix of tradition with modernity. While Chapels tend to attract persons occupying a similar stratum, parishioners and visitors of Bon Pasteur come from surrounding rich and poor neighborhoods. Its "Babel" of language, class, music, represents everyday life in Cotonou. Here and elsewhere, the diversity and interaction would make difficult any attempt to sift through the habiti (or practices) of a single religious imagination. Though on occasions tradition seems to prevail, it is more a give and take as a slow dance of tradition with modernity.

There are many more such examples of lived Catholicism in Benin, for example the procession of Christ the King when a crowd accompanied by priests walks the streets, dancing to tam-tams and other instruments. The crowd, both hands in the air sometimes heard yelling "Vive Jesus" [long live Jesus], surrounds several priests, one of them holding the Blessed Sacrament under a large colorful umbrella traditionally held over kings. At each corner of the road are decorated altars where the procession stops for prayers. These are called *reposoir* because the Blessed Sacrament is placed on each altar for a *repos* (rest).

According to one anthropologist, street corner stops have traditional religious significance. In Vodun, offerings to divinities are typically made at street corners. Catholic processions stop here to modify this traditional meaning and show Christ everywhere including street corners. Here again, is the presence of tradition in lived Catholicism. Past and present interact. Collective memory gives relevance to this action. What happens in processions is not syncretism because at least at the macro, it is empty of elements that conflict with the basic tenets of Catholicism. In these examples, the faithful are called to use elements of their culture to make Catholicism meaningful. It is inculturation at best, though this attention to street corners could also be interpreted as a form of competition in an attempt to counter traditional religion.

Tradition and modernity: the respondents speak

Whether discussing rituals or other aspects of their culture, the respondents raise this issue of interaction between tradition and modernity. Their comments guide our search for understanding the Catholic imagination and what at first appears syncretism. The interviews provide many insights into this "tradi-modern" encounter, but I find particularly helpful one personal account of religious trajectory, from a mix of Islam with Vodun and Catholicism, to Catholicism, and eventually the Catholic priesthood.

The respondent was recommended by someone who knew his life history well, and thought it would offer important information not only about the life of an individual, but also popular Catholicism in Benin. The interview took place in the respondent's office. He sat at his desk and I across from him. He was warm, welcoming, clearly interested in the topic and looking to share information. Born of Muslim parents, he experienced a mix of religion early within his own family.

> As all good Beninese, and as all Africans, there was a . . . family environment of syncretism between Catholic faith—for those who were Catholic because there were Catholics in the family—and the Vaudou religion. In the family, there were also Muslims who syncretized with Vaudou.

His maternal grandmother was Catholic but mother converted to Islam before his birth. Mother and father practiced Islam while for a few months, the young boy attended Koran school. Despite this Islamic training, his relationship with grandmother was close and he visited her often. But there were also limits on their relationship. "My grandmother had a great deal of respect for my religion since, when she was going to Mass, she would take me back to my parents . . . so I would not have to go." One might question the idea of "my religion" in this situation. What could it be? Despite their multiple belonging, the family identifies with Islam and it would seem safe to assume that "my religion" means Islam.

One day, the respondent asked his grandmother if he could accompany her to Mass. She agreed.

> The priest celebrated Mass, it was a white missionary priest . . . . When it came time for communion, my grandmother stood up to go take communion . . . . I followed, but was made to return quietly to my seat. On the way out grandmother explained to me that it was necessary to learn catechism before being able to take 'the little host.'

Sometimes, during his interview, the respondent speaking as the child he was then, referred to the Eucharist as "little host" and "little biscuit." He remained puzzled by the "big host" and wanted to know why only the celebrant could be so lucky to have that.

> My grandmother explained that a special catechism that the priest learned authorized him to receive communion with the "big host." . . . So I said, if I have to become Catholic, I am going to learn the catechism to receive communion with the "big host." . . . Grandmother laughed. That has stayed with me.

From time to time, the respondent follows grandmother to Church and eventually becomes an altar boy. Still officially Muslim, he visits the Mosque but whenever possible also serves Mass on Sundays. In his own words, "I was doing three things at the same time: I was a Muslim, a Catholic and I was in the Vaudou . . . because at home they were doing Vaudou."

Overtime as his interest grows in the Catholic faith, he begins studying more but without letting go of Islam. "I went to the Mosquée when I wanted, especially on feast days . . . Ramadan . . . . I went to pray with the people." However, when called to the family house for a traditional ceremony, "I am again ready . . . we did it all the time." So, the respondent engages in a *va-et-vient* (coming-and-going) between one religious practice . . . and another . . . and another. To him, these practices are a normal part of everyday life.

It is in his third year of catechism that the respondent decides to break with Islam. "I chose, but not without difficulty . . . . because my Muslim parents did not want this . . . my father was different." However, father approves the switch, because "I had come to be so attached to my maternal grandmother." But on the other hand, mother feeling responsible blames herself because her son's closeness to her Catholic mother (his grandmother) has triggered his rejection of Islam—religion of his father. Following the switch to Catholicism, the respondent goes on to live with grandmother, is baptized and receives his first communion. "Well, that is the way that I became a Catholic."

There is more to the trajectory. While officially severing ties with Islam and becoming Catholic, the respondent continues practicing traditional religion: "When I was at my house and there were ceremonies, they called me. I did not see this as a problem. I would go . . . and I would do the ceremonies with them." With this come-and-go between one and the other religion, his next step on the religious road is unexpected.

> I felt within me the desire to become priest and to do as the priest was doing at the altar. . . . And so I nurtured that, I spoke about that. . . . I had to take a test . . . and then I was retained to start at the seminary. . . . . Once in the seminary, I finally turned my back on everything practiced by the Vaudou religion and . . . . today, I am happy to serve as priest at this parish. Here it is . . . . the story of my formation.

But this story seems more than one of formation. It comes closer to a transformation. It is a story of conversion. Besides describing his personal trajectory, the respondent offers it as a model for the marriage of tradition with modernity in Benin. Having experienced multiple religious roads himself, and served as Pastor of a local parish where he counseled parishioners, he speaks authoritatively about the Beninese imagination but rejects the idea that Catholicism in Benin is mixed. "Mixing" is not an accurate term. "Mixing" causes him a certain discomfort, even as "It is true that, with the Second Vatican Council, we have to live our faith as part of our identity, and there is the movement of inculturation . . . .the welcoming of Christ in our culture."

But if not a *mix* of tradition and modernity, what exactly means "living our faith as part of our identity"? At least in the southern region of that country, Vaudou, the traditional religion is part of Beninese identity. Is it not also a part of Catholic identity? Perhaps, it is first necessary to describe Vaudou, and explain the place it occupies in Beninese culture. But rather than a dictionary definition of Vaudou, I turn to the respondent's own, helpful not only in understanding what it means to be an adept but also one consequence of belonging. The description will surprise many especially in the Western world who in their heads carry a different image of the Vaudou religion.

Vaudou: intuition and system.

Dolls and pins are the image of Vaudou in the minds of many Americans. Prior to visiting Benin, I myself carried that image. Often we hear the phrase "Voodoo economics" and other associations which point to an ethnocentric view of African religion. It is with this in mind that I suggest the following definition of Vaudou to be unfamiliar to many Western readers.

> Man, whoever he may be, at one point, is awaken to the presence, the existence of God in the world . . . and he tries to meet this God. . . . marches to seek God, and the search turned into this religion . . . named Vaudou. . . . He searches for God. . . . He searches that which goes beyond. He does not find it directly. He finds it through intermediaries that I will call manifestations of the sacred and the divine.

The respondent finds his description closely related to that of Beninese philosopher and theologian Barthélemy Adoukonou for whom Vaudou is "the cult of our most precious memories." Further, in this cult, the respondent explains "it is our grandparents we adore. . . . That is one dimension of traditional religion. . . .What did the grandparents adore?" he asks. "They adored those . . . who loved them, those who adored them, those who created in them sacred forces and manifested the divine." But, he cautions, "it is not yet God. It is only a manifestation."

Other religions might substitute the word "honor" for "adore." For example "honor thy mother and father" instead of "adore thy mother and father" since only God is worthy of adoration. Too, the command to "honor" might be extended to grandparents and all others who love us, have loved us, who may be considered extensions of mother and father thus manifestations of the divine. The emphasis on "honor" instead of "adore" seems the one separating traditional religion from Christian Catholicism. There are many other manifestations of the divine, for example in the natural world—trees, rivers and animals and the entire metaphysical world also to be honored—not adored.

The respondent illustrates this idea of manifestation of the divine to be adored using the example of a giant, impressive tree.

> The divine manifest itself . . . and I kneel, and in this tree I adore the one I call God. . . . I request things. But I do not get what I ask. . . . . Worst, this tree that I adore, someone else could come and cut it. . . . He comes and cuts the tree that I . . . consider sacred. . . . . The tree says nothing. It lets itself be cut. I am going to be shocked. So I do not want another to destroy what I myself take as object of my faith. I am going to take measures of security to protect what I adore. . . .

I can also take measures to make my religion efficacious. When I begin to do that, I am no longer advancing. I stopped on the road. Or may be I think that I have come to the end of the road. When I stop, I begin to set foot on a system.

There is a difference between the intuited divine which is the beginning of religion and a religious system he describes as human intervention that gives intuited religion its content and efficacy. Once a system develops, the march stops. "The system that I start, it is I that gives it its content. And the content that I give this system . . . [makes it] that my quest is completely spoiled. That is the system Vaudou."

Thus is the difference between traditional religion as intuition and as system. The respondent labels the intuition stage positive and the system stage negative. "I repeat what I said."

The religion Vaudou is two things in the context of syncretism that we are discussing. There is a religion Vaudou that I call "Vaudou positif," and there is "Vaudou negatif.". . . What is positive is this push that I have that is not yet a cult, and is not yet crystallized in a cult, and I can call it sacred. . . . I have an intuition that there is something sacred that exists, that can be found in the world. And I search for that something sacred . . . then I begin acting. This action can inspire my religious attitudes, that is, the movements, ways of adoring. But normally, support of my adoration is not an end in itself. It is that religion I call "Vaudou positif," in the sense that it explains our intuition, our quest for God.

This intuition stage inspires certain rituals and practices that enhance adoration of the divine through manifestations. Intuition continues the quest. Intuition is positive. When then does intuition become negative? Where is the line between positive and negative?

It is negative when this quest transforms itself progressively into a system of cult. This system is founded on efficacy, a little magic, and thus it is a system that today is called the Vaudou religion. It is a closed system. It is not open to accept other things. That is why when one speaks of Christ, the one who is in the system Vaudou rejects it.

It is a system open only to itself which "does not accept evangelization. It does not accept that it is shown Christ. And when you advance Christ, it does not accept adherence to Christ. . . ." Such a systematic, hermetic system suggests no possible mix of religion, hence the respondent's discomfort with the term "mixing" and any suggestion that it might describe relations between this traditional system and Catholicism. Mixing is not possible because, as he puts it, the traditional system is closed.

When it is like that, it is not possible to mix . . . because Vaudou expresses a will for power that one carries within . . . . What is positive in Vaudou is this intuition that has put us on the road, and that makes us respect the sacred. That

is what the [Catholic] Church pulls from the faithful. . . . Everyone has this tendency of looking for the divine, of looking for God. . . . Everyone everywhere
has that. It is not only men of Vaudou.

"That is what the Church pulls from the faithful." It is the positive aspect of
Vaudou. It is the intuition of sacred. And, in that regard, there does not seem a
huge difference between intuition and the Catholic imagination. Marching continues in the quest for what is thought to be beyond.

> Well now, each has his manner of living . . . according to dispositions of hour,
> and time, and according to cultural elements that he has. So when the Church
> takes man, it takes him entirely. It . . . keeps what in him has always pushed
> him to seek God. That is why, for example, the Catholic Church, in its concern
> to let the Beninese man live his faith completely and feel himself really Chris-
> tian while being African, keeps the elements that . . . are positive elements and
> that are not elements necessarily taken advantages by the system. The Church
> revalorizes these elements.

The Church does not separate a believer from his/her culture. It hopes to retain
the positive, intuitive aspect of traditional religion. What the Church attempts to
eliminate, are its negative aspects—the traditional system. There can be no mix
of Vaudou and Catholicism, if by Vaudou one means the traditional system. "I
do not know if I have made an effort to show what I think of intuition and com-
prehension in this domain. So, for me, that is it. So when it is this, to say that the
Church mixes Vaudou, is wrong. . . . We would not accept."

"We" means the Church, the hierarchy, the macrolevel. Based upon the respondent's explanation, and distinction between positive and negative, it is possible to imagine the Catholic imagination mixed, if not with the system, with the
Vaudou positif which precedes that system. Why? Because if what the respondent calls positive is only an intuition, that is a quest for God dressed in the cultural garb, the Catholic imagination too will "match that outfit" because nurtured
and nurturing in the same environment.

If Vaudou positif—or the quest and intuition—is a form of spirituality, was
it not shared with missionaries who believed in something greater than themselves? The quest and intuition merge tradition and modernity. And indeed, at
the very beginning of their encounters, missionaries and colonizers shared (or
pretended to share) this spirituality with the colonized. But one needs also be
careful. Though missionaries and colonizers were Europeans and it is said missionaries were often instruments for colonizers, the intention here is not to con-
found them as their motivations were apparently different in many ways. Missionaries came for evangelization while colonizers came after land and other
resources.

The respondent hints at the nature of this Catholic imagination in Benin.
He is clear and definitive that: "You cannot mix Vaudou and Catholic Christianity. It is not possible. It is in fact two different things." As he differentiates between intuition and system, he concludes the system incompatible with Catholi-

cism but the intuition and quest possibly retained. He also differentiates between inculturation and mixing. "Inculturation is not a mix." As he puts it, "incultura-tion is the welcoming of Christ by our cultures. . . . We are born in a specific culture." Inculturation seeks to include in Catholicism, the quest and intuition in their traditional forms. In other words, popular Catholicism in Benin uses "pieces" of tradition, but only those pieces that fit the larger puzzle.

Health and illness: fear of system

Fear is rampant in Beninese society. And explaining further the differentiation between positive and negative, it is possible to advance that fear is triggered by what the respondent portrays as system—or the negative side of traditional relig-ion. In a newspaper article on the values, hopes and threats of the family in Af-rica, the Beninese scholar and Catholic priest Philippe Kinkpon explains wide-spread fear in this way: "If a child has diarrhea, immediately one thinks of bewitchment caused by a family member suspected of sorcery. This [thinking] nurtures a climate of suspicion and fear within the family structure. 'The real enemy is not elsewhere, he is in your family' is often heard."[21]

While I was in Benin, a man in his early 40s suddenly becomes ill. Ruling out the possibility of his health improving, modern medicine condemns him to death. But he and his family go elsewhere, since they believe his illness pro-voked by a close relative they are convinced dislikes him. They think they can change the course of the disease, get to the source whatever it may be—and "turn it around." They consult a well-known priest exorcist. Despite the medical diagnosis and until the moment he died, the family has faith that his health will improve.

At the man's Catholic funeral, one of the eulogies pointed to the unusual nature of his ailment and premature passing. There are many similar cases in Benin where suspicion and fear of the other is everyday life. Death is never natural. Even in old age the Beninese will question the occurrence of death and attribute it to some human intervention.

The fear of being poisoned is constant even when giving or accepting a handshake in a culture where this gesture signifies respect (see Quénum and St. Jean, 2008). Water, considered the best drink is an important sign of welcome and, after a handshake, the very first offered a visitor. Yet, drinking water too provokes fear of being harmed. One is advised to be careful where and what one eats or drinks. There are fears of direct attacks on one's health but people also wary of indirect such attacks. They fear that "un sort" could be "sent" to them, a fear by the way far from paranoia, grounded in everyday reality especially that of family life, as Kinkpon puts it (Quénum and St. Jean, 2008). That is why, in an effort to understand the Beninese context of the Catholic imagination, it is also important to discuss provoked illness and the fear it creates, as well tradi-tional medicine, for Beninese people regardless of religious affiliation represents one solution. According to informants, a discussion of the Catholic imagination leads naturally to discussions of traditional religion, which lead to discussions of tradi-therapy and to pharmacopée—one of its branches.

Illness and cure

My own research suggests that the respondents' assessment of the link between Catholicism and traditional religion is correct. I went to Benin to study the Catholic imagination without any intention of going beyond it. My intention was to interview Catholics only—cradle[22] and convert—as I did in previous years in the Midwest. This was naïve on my part. During the first year of my visit to Benin, I quickly realized from speaking to informants that to understand the Catholic imagination, I would need also understanding traditional religion.

The respondent above goes one step further and suggests "to understand Beninese Catholicism, it is also important to understand pharmacopée." Tradi-therapy of which pharmacopée is one branch cannot be separated from traditional religion, thus the necessity to grasp its meaning for the people in Benin—still in an attempt to understand the Catholic imagination.

> There are some . . . Christians who confront certain problems. . . . They prefer to find solutions at the tradi-therapists, the traditional healers, rather than come to church. . . . To understand Beninese Catholicism, it is also important to understand pharmacopée . . . an element in traditional medicine. . . . And, from here, from all of this, you will be able to single out the imagination. If you speak of Vaudou and you do not speak of traditional medicine, you have not said anything yet, because you are speaking of problems of fear. . . . So when you have defended all of that . . . it allows you to arrive at convincing, reliable conclusions.

Here is a solid outline for the present discussion. And indeed, prior to this interview, I had the opportunity to speak to an expert of pharmacopée. A colleague of mine, close friend of this expert, arranged for a meeting at the interviewee's home outside of Cotonou.

I seat with this expert in his living room, listening carefully as he defines the art of treating illnesses with plants, speaks about the beginnings of his involvement with this field and how he acquired his knowledge. At about age 20, he found himself in a work setting where older co-workers practiced pharmacopée without hiding from him the exact proportions of ingredients. Relatively young at the time, he was not perceived by other workers as posing a threat. But in silence he observed carefully, absorbed and later impressed many outside the work setting as he applied this knowledge. Word spread about his talents which earned him an invitation to join a plant treatment health Center. "J'ai donné tous les secrets. Tout. Je n'ai rien gardé" (I gave all of my secrets [to the Center] everything). I kept nothing. I am Christian, I am Christian. I kept nothing. I kept nothing.

Why a person suffering from an illness would choose this expert over a traditional healer? His response was, often people consulting him have tried modern forms of treatment, but not having found satisfaction turn to pharmacopée as a last resort. There are also other reasons for this choice, including the cost of modern medicine and loyalty to one's religious beliefs. General pharmacopée costs less than modern medicine. Moreover, those seeking help from him prefer someone who shares their Catholic faith. Sometimes, the sick will use both modern medicine and pharmacopée simultaneously—just in case.

As I am curious to know specifically what traditional healers do that the respondent does not and what he does they do not do, he explains healers use symbols—oils, heads of animals . . . have words and incantations, invoke spirits. He explains his own position, complains about these rituals and other behaviors engaged in by some of his traditional healer friends.

> I have friends, Vaudounon friends . . . who have not successfully healed this person or that person, and they turn to me to ask me for advice and formulae. I give them advice and the formulae. They take my formulae and, instead of giving them directly to the sick, first they put it on the Vaudou and tell the sick 'you have to take a goat, and you have to take . . . and you have to take, and you have to take.' They do that to live, to eat.

I suggested to him that traditional healers have a right to ask their patients for money, as he himself probably does. The request of traditional healers for payment represents a fee for services rendered—a rebuke with which he agreed.

> But ancient tradition is secret and these healers live of deceit, of lies . . . making people spend first before giving the medicine that is necessary. . . . And all of this is to have a lot of money to live on. . . . There are certain among them who can see things, and others . . . consult the fâ. . . . But I do not see. . . . If you have pain I will ask you questions. . . . Tell me the story of your disease, et cetera, et cetera.

As the respondent sees it, his own approach to treatment is different from that of traditional healers and comparable to modern medicine. He provides an example of the way in which he interacts with patients.

> A woman was brought to me. She has never had children. She is [in her late 30s]. I ask questions: how old was she when she got married, do her periods come normally. I ask lots of questions. Has she had [lab] analyses? What did the doctor say? Has her husband had a spermogram? So, from here, there is a point that does not work. He must do the spermogram. They have to go back and get the results together. . . . But the husband took the results alone three years ago and the wife is not aware of them. Does the husband have a child elsewhere? She said no. I say, I can only treat you if your husband agrees to give the results of the spermogram. I am not a magician. I have to identify the illness before I can treat it. The husband did not come.

Still critical of healers, the respondent suggests "If it were a traditional healer . .
. even though he knows that he cannot, he is going to make them spend, and the
result is null but they will spend. That is all. And, when they [the clients] are
tired, they are going to leave." Some might argue the unethical behavior described sounds too much like that of some physicians in the western medical
profession. Nevertheless, the respondent contrasts with his own approach to
treatment which he says is scientific, methodical, ethical, and successful in cur-
ing a number of illness, including sterility, typhoid fever, malaria, rheumatism,
paralyses, and more. With pharmacopée "I have successfully healed all of that."

Where does he find plants for clients? He looks for them in nature. "Some
plants treat fever. . . . Some . . . cure malaria, fatigue, sterility." He showed me
some of the plants in his yard, described the properties of each, in what circumstances they are used, what they do and why they do it. Started by the late Monsignor de Souza, this Center for Health in the heart of Cotonou is affiliated with
the Catholic Church and open to everyone regardless of religious affiliation.

Again, to understand traditional medicine one must understand traditional
religion and vice versa. And since this and previous chapters argued even a superficial knowledge of tradition can help understand the Catholic imagination,
knowledge of traditional medicine is also helpful in this regard. As the tradi-
therapist shares his views, he sounds much like another respondent who earlier
in this chapter spoke of his multiple religious trajectories. Starting with traditional religion, he too explains the link with pharmacopée.

> While I am not a specialist of Vaudou, I can say a few words on traditional re-
> ligion. . . . A man looking for God has invented divinities who serve as inter-
> mediaries between man and God. These divinities are often places of venera-
> tion, and offered sacrifices to obtain favors of them. Healers use the same . . . to
> ask for favors and heal humans. In saying that it is not the virtues of plants that
> are going to heal, but the intercession of divinities, healers associate the two.
> This also allows them to do some obscurantism and to eat. . . . So there is
> money, and there are animals, that are brought to them. . . . Healers have to eat.
> . . And so, it is not only the properties of plants that healers use to cure people.
> They say, well, we are going also to ask the intercession of divinities, and di-
> vinities solicit animals, food . . . This is to have effectively a lot of money to
> feed their family.

With traditional healers, more is involved in the treatment process. That is why
the Catholic Church wanted to demystify the process and spread knowledge that
plants have natural virtues.

> It is the Catholic Church that said we can purify these ways of doing . . . that
> plants . . . can heal without having recourse to divinities. . . . So it is here that
> the Catholic can be helpful in saying, it is possible to select, . . . to put what is
> in nature on one side, and what is spiritual and obscurantism, fetishism on the
> other side, so that there is no mix. In this way . . . of phytotherapy, the Church
> allows Christians to heal people without fetishism, without animal sacrifices. . .
> . No mixing of that . . . so . . . this is part of the effort of inculturation.

Inculturation is one goal of the treatment center which opened for the first time after the Synod at the request of participants:

> It is Christians themselves who asked that traditional values in the medical world not be completely swept away, and it is possible to select what is good from the tradition, if only in the area of phytotherapy, the virtue of plants. . . These can be utilized while staying Christian, without having to seek help from healers. . . . Now we can have Christians who do not seek help from fetish . . . from obscurantism, who know plants . . . know natural medicine, and can use them. . . . So it is because of the synod . . . the bishops and Christians of the Diocese of Cotonou have reflected on this. . . . [Christians] asked the bishops if there are Christians . . . competent in this domain, that they be called . . . to share their knowledge and put it toward the good of the Church, the good of Christians, without them seeking help from other fetish. . . It is to avoid amalgam. It is to avoid syncretism. This is to avoid [people] say[ing] 'we are going to Mass on Sunday, we are all for baptisms, communions but, at night, we are ready to go to the fetish, to the traditional healers, because [modern] medicine cannot treat our [provoked] illness.'

As discussed earlier, many illnesses thought to be provoked drive the sick to traditional healers. It is not paranoia. Most respondents agree that "it is true provoked illnesses exist." What then is the role of pharmacopée in case of an illness thought to have been provoked?

> pharmacopée listens to discover the story of the illness, to identify . . . its origins. Is the disease really . . . ordinary. . .? In our hospitals . . . doctors who after [lab] analyses . . . cannot find a [cause for a] disease will say, "Really we have done everything as far as modern medicine is concerned. . . . We have arrived at destination so, sorry, go look for medicine in the traditional world."

At times it is physicians themselves, the practitioners of modern medicine who send clients in desperate situations to traditional healers, when they think modern medicine has gone as far as possible and is not doing what it is expected.

> When you get there, and the people are sick, what do they do? They go to the fetish; they go to the *bokonon,* as these people are called. They say to them . . . "We are sick, but we have not been able to heal. Help us." And so, for [these *bokonon*], it is sometimes easy to justify mak[ing] these people spend lots of money. . . . The priests . . . bring to me the faithful who find themselves in a difficult situation. . . . They orient these people to the Center.

Thus, pharmacopée (also called phyto-therapy, one form of tradi-therapy) is an alternative to traditional healing medicine and an important form of inculturation. Clearly, from the view of this respondent, inculturation is different from mixing. And to explain the difference, he uses the value of fidelity.

> Before the Holy Sacrament . . . I am able to feel something mysterious happening, and I can stay in that fervor. It is a good thing. One can inculturat[e] what traditional religion has already given to us [fidelity]. . . . A liturgy of Vaudou that has taught us rigor, fidelity . . . fidelity. . . . because we are afraid. We are afraid of death. Vaudou threatens us with death, if we are not faithful.

Fidelity is a good thing, according to this respondent. And fidelity a value already cultivated in traditional religion is compatible with Catholicism. The value of fidelity can be inculturated. The difference is in the motivation for fidelity. Traditional religion's motivation for fidelity is incompatible because it is based upon the fear of divinities. Fidelity, the outcome of fear, is different from fidelity, outcome of love. Only the latter can be inculturated because only the latter is compatible with Catholicism. There is no mixing. As the respondent puts it, "It would be necessary to change the mentality, keep the fidelity . . . because God loves us, and I cannot deceive the one who loves me, and died for me." This analogy explains the difference between mix and inculturation which is more fluid and complex.

Besides tradi-therapy, and values such as fidelity, there are many other areas of potential inculturation. One is the area of liturgical songs:

> The songs that we have and . . . execute . . . for us they are sacred rhythms. . . .
> I was speaking of . . . Vaudou songs. . . . We think that [these songs] are sacred.
> . . . To give honor and homage, we have had the intuition to create what we call
> . . . sacred rhythms. . . . The sacred rhythm says something and explains something. One can go from this rhythm and compose (Christian) religious songs. . .
> . One feels that what is being said is religious.

How can traditional religious songs be inculturated? This too seems a complex project.

> You have to evangelize these rhythms because the tam tam . . . says something that is typically Vaudou. This [something] can be changed with the words of the gospel. It is not necessary to invent something else. What we already know . . . I would say, determines our fibers, and then . . . . can be conserved. We keep them, but we keep them while welcoming Christ . . . . into it. . . . And when one sings, that is expressive. It says something.

Not all approve the project of inculturating traditional songs. In addition to the issue of rhythm, some will see inculturation as equivalent to "stealing" or plagiarizing the tradition.

> Some [chiefs of traditional religion] think that we [Catholics] are only copying what they are already doing. But I think it is an error. We are all at the same point of departure. The fact is that we have walked together until a certain level. We were going somewhere. At one point we lost sight of where we were going. And we stopped there to express all our being, all that we are. And what we found has been called Vaudou.

There is no plagiarism some say. When a new element is introduced and cultural change occurs, the old cultural life cannot be completely discarded explains the respondent:

> And it happens that someone found the light and . . . he takes what he has, and leaves with it. That's it. So, in moving ahead . . . he lets go of everything that has no value, and, that which is of value he keeps. Otherwise, he would be up-rooted. . . . Thus it is necessary to be rooted somewhere, and . . . to the extent that he is sufficiently rooted in his culture . . . he can return to see the people from his culture . . . speak to them in the language he knows, and be able to convince them, and help them encounter Christ.

Even while grasping modernity, it is important to remain rooted in traditional culture. But remaining rooted also presents a risk which requires caution.

> I have told you, do not lose sight of what I have said; there is a system that has put itself in place . . . that is close and . . . cannot receive something from else-where. Those who try to get out are kept from doing so. But because what makes them leave is stronger than what keeps them from leaving, they leave anyway. It is they who become Christians . . . and return to evangelize the set-ting.

In other words, one must be careful to remain in the cultural quest and intuition—not the system. Those who stay in this system and mix it with Catholicism do so because of the threat of death. "They risk death. . . but one must not be afraid of dying because the blood of martyrs is fertilizer? Some know it . . . and because they refuse to be martyrs they use syncretism." Again, one sees the difference between mixing and inculturation.

Inculturation is important to the faithful. When two traditions meet, if no inculturation takes place,

> it is to say that everything that I lived is swept aside. I throw it away. But if he is with you and does not feel at ease, he does not feel at ease because he feels you are a foreigner, and you tell him to marry, to marry all of your ways and to let go his ways of doing . . . So to please you, he acts as if he was with you but he is not convinced.

This sounds to me like the issue of double consciousness that occupied W.E.B. Du Bois. It also reminds of the journalist Leonita McClain who speaks of having "one foot in each world."[23] The outcome of assimilation is emptiness.

> He feels emptiness after this concubinage . . . that is it. Do you see what I am saying? . . . The person cannot live in a frank manner, and that is what has cre-ated the syncretism from the start of the encounter between the Vaudou religion and Christianity. And this syncretism has stayed a long time and it has become natural, it has become evident for the people. . . . People do not see that life can be different. And we have functioned in that way, we have done catechism, the

catechism, well everybody lives in this way. What makes it that today this continues and that . . . regardless of major efforts of inculturation that are made the
people remain attached.

Cultural "emptiness" may be likened to a state of anomie where things no longer
make sense for the uprooted. People need to remain grounded in their culture
even when embracing a new one. The need for cultural roots explains the historical persistence of syncretism of traditional religion and Catholicism in West
Africa—one foot in each religious world. The need to remain grounded is one
reason why efforts at inculturation have been slow. While the Catholic Church
does not support mixing, the people still do. Thus, there is a need for more studies of traditional culture and religion aimed at separating compatible from elements deemed incompatible. These studies are a first step toward a successful
inculturation of the positive tradition (positive as defined by the respondent).

> So, when I say the responsibility is shared, there has been this first level of in-
> sufficiency, the second where we, as priest . . . the clergy, autochthones . . . a
> lot of people have received the faith, we have to be able to take back the cate-
> cheses in hand while taking account of all of that. The effort is timid. It is slow.
> It is not taking, because it needs investment, it needs people who work, who are
> doing research to know our culture better, and to know what language to speak
> to the people of this culture. Well, it is not entirely absent but it is timid.

That the Beninese is a Métis is also an interesting suggestion. Métis (or metissage) refers to someone of mixed ancestry. It also suggests duality. Beninese
culture is a metissage of tradition and modernity whose elements and the potential for duality must be understood before successful inculturation. "The . . . Beninese today is . . . a cultural Métis. On the cultural level he is a Métis. He is
nowhere most of the time. He is nowhere . . . because he does not know his culture; he does not master the realities of his culture."

Emphasis here is on knowledge of culture. Without this knowledge, the
Beninese suffers from a state of anomie, the feeling of displacement, the sense
of being in no specific place. It is important thus, while embracing a new way of
life, that one continues to be rooted. "But since in men there is something profound that calls him to recognize the presence of the sacred and the mysticism of
life, as soon as there is a problem he has to run to the healers, to the charlatans
and others to be protected."

Everyone holds an intuition of the sacred, earlier called spirituality. The
need to be culturally rooted drives people back to the tradition, even if not ap-
proved by the other sides of their métis make-up.

> Well, that does not keep them from being Christians, to be in church every
> Sunday. It does not keep them from seeking spiritual security in esoteric
> lodges. Well, those who are in the traditional religion and are rooted in it, they
> have lived the traditional religion, but they have not studied. There are those
> who live traditional religion without knowing completely what it is.

This mix of tradition and modernity is due to lack of knowledge of the tradition. Adepts of Vaudou live their religion, but do not completely understand it. Religious tradition is transmitted from generation to generation without being questioned by its inheritors. The beliefs are taken for granted. It is like being moved by faith. As one respondent puts it, "My father did it and the tradition was transmitted to me. I continue to do what father has done and that's all. And these people are dangerous."

So, from generation to generation tradition is transmitted. And since tradition is mixed with Catholic education (modernity), mixing at the micro level seems inevitable. Indeed the respondents own words suggest a sort of duality originating from the coexistence of compatible with incompatible elements in everyday life. Given this metissage, inculturation, an ideal from the point of view of the Church, might be difficult to achieve.

Problems Associated with Inculturation.

An interview with a female physician highlights further the distinction between mixing and inculturation, as well as problems associated with inculturation.

The respondent is a cradle Catholic and strict adherent to rules of the Church—even when in countries like the United States, some of these rules continue provoking resistance from practicing and cultural Catholics.[24] For example, the respondent supports the idea of a male-only priesthood and insists, "There is nothing in the world that would make me leave the Catholic Church—that is a profound conviction."

When the respondent was growing up, her parents also fervent Catholics, made sure she practiced her faith (or should it be "their faith?"). Later on, her involvement in the charismatic movement helped strengthen this ascribed religious identity. She speaks of her love of the hierarchy and disagreement with western women who want to be priest. "What I like most in the Catholic Church is the hierarchy and obedience of the hierarchy that is really a stability in this religion, and it inspires a lot of respect . . . from the entire world." The male gender prerequisite for the priesthood does not constitute a barrier to her faith. When younger, she told a priest she would be a nun only if nuns were allowed to celebrate Mass to which the priest replied, "If you are waiting for that, you are not needed." They both laughed. Today, she still laughs about that comment.

As she became more knowledgeable of her faith, she gained a superior understanding of the expectations of the Church for women.

> For me, it is not the fact of celebrating the Eucharist that opens the doors of heaven. . . . [For] it is possible to gain salvation in other ways. . . . There are thousands of ways to serve the Lord. And what made me even happier, is when I read the encyclical of John Paul II on the dignity of women. I discovered the place where a woman belongs. . . . I have no desire to be priest or priestess . . .[or] to say Mass.

The respondent visits other churches only on special occasions.

> If it is the relative of a friend from a different religion who died and there is a
> funeral service, if it is a baptism, and you are invited . . . to show solidarity . . .
> support. That's all. Once I prayed with Pentecostals at an ecumenical service. . .
> . I went there in a spirit of openness.

Hence her strict loyalty and deep involvement in the Church give additional value to her views on mixing. She believes the hierarchy does not mix but
admits,

> The majority of baptized, when being challenged, think . . . Catholicism alone
> cannot solve their problems. So it is in addition to prayers that they do, they
> search for other solutions, they search for help in traditional religion, in the
> practices, it is not in the traditional religion but in the traditional practices. That
> is . . . what is of the culture.

Most people do not have complete faith in prayer alone and do whatever
they can, whatever it takes, to be sure of solving their problems. If a "child .
. . is gravely ill,"

> one goes to the hospital and, at the same time, . . . to see a healer to help treat or
> exorcize, and so forth, the ill. The problem is, this same healer could be chief of
> cult. In other words, sometimes the one responsible for a cult of traditional re-
> ligion is also a healer.

But this comment also highlights the complexity of separating one set of roles
and practices from another. Healer and chief of traditional religion are often
combined. One comes with the other. Yet, for Catholics, the combination of
these statuses and roles presents a risk.

> The risk [for Catholics] is where one is not able to set boundaries because this
> healer will not separate his knowledge of plants from his practice of Vaudou.
> And immediately, you no longer know if it is the Vaudou that heals, or if it is
> the knowledge of plants since, . . . he could ask you to make some offerings to
> his Vaudou in addition to the medicine that he gives you. Then . . . one can no
> longer distinguish immediately. . . . That is the case for most Beninese.

The situation creates confusion (another case of anomie) for the person seeking
help. Yet, little can they do to avoid it. Societal circumstances influenced their
choice. The healer may offer the additional spiritual help that the one practicing
pharmacopée alone is thought not to offer.

> They are always worried, worried of something, worried about the future, wor-
> ried of their own health, worried of the health of their children or a relative,

worried about the material, worried about their mobility—social, political, or occupational.

Sacrifices to divinities is the point of transition from one faith to the other. Once sacrifices are offered, cultural practices become religious practices. Catholics who offer sacrifices to divinities are "mixing" religious practices. The offering of sacrifice goes beyond inculturation.

As indicated earlier, the physician herself does not mix practices, but during her primary socialization she remembers a habit of mixing in her family home

> I was born in a Catholic family. . . . But, we lived nevertheless a certain mix. My father, at home . . . there is the Vaudou. . . . Also, my parents took us to the healers. . . . Some healers are at the same time responsible of Vaudou, so it has already happened . . . that we find ourselves . . . in front of a Vaudou, or . . . one had to make offerings when I was little. . . . The cult of the ancestors means that . . . in fact, the dead are not dead and that they will always be with us.

Things have changed from the time she left home for the university, "Okay, since I became a student I was made to discover Christ . . . . I would not do this [mixing] for anything in the world." She remembers her parents moving comfortably from one side of their religious faith to the other. But, her own faith today is transformed from this primary socialization. She goes further explaining, what sometimes may be interpreted as a mix of religious practices are only survivals of the tradition in everyday life. The practices do not necessarily have religious significance nor do they represent mixing. For example, another name for Vaudou is "*Revenant.*" To say that the "Revenants are out," one might say, the "Vaudou are out." But even as the Revenant plays a role in traditional religion, he is also an important part of the culture. The presence of a Revenant in the home does not necessarily amount to syncretism.

> And then . . . in the family when someone dies, well, that person ['s body] in principle must . . . will go . . . to church, will be given all sacraments but at the same time, the Revenant will come and pray on the body and so forth, and close the coffin before going to the Church because it is the practice in the family. After the funeral, there are ceremonies that the Revenant will come to, for example the 41st day after the funeral, that is the dead is symbolized by something called *assin.* I don't know if you have already seen this, it is represented by . . . that is the *forgerons* [blacksmiths] who make this wreath and one foot, and then during 41 days what has represented this dead person stays in the house of the dead. One prays often . . . one puts this [representation] in a bedroom, there is one light that always stays lighted, close, close, close, close to this thing and represents the dead. One does prayers often there, traditional prayers. There are traditional rituals and then on the 41st day, the Revenant is going . . . to come and get this . . . and take it to the family home in a place where are [buried] all [members] from the family who have died. So they are going to make him enter in his family where the [other] members have gone be-

fore him. So this is to say it is true that I am in a Catholic family . . . but there is
this family ritual that exists relative to the cult of the dead.

This is a religious ritual. But it is also a cultural practice. The respondent shares
even more of what happens during these rituals, "There are other things in the
ritual of the dead. There is a ceremony that is done on the third day and seventh
day." Notice the numbers whose source the respondent questions, because found
in both Catholicism and Vaudou.

Okay, the numbers 3 and 7 are numbers that are complete in the Catholic religion, that is, as an intellectual, I am asking questions. These are people who have
not been baptized in the Church. Why is it that the numbers 3, 7, and 40 are so
important to them? And then, well, I conclude that we are all children of the
same Father whether we want it or not, every human is born of God and the
Lord himself inspires his children as he wants it, opens to their intelligence a
number of things visible, and maybe each understands and practices in his own
way.

The respondent offers a religious explanation for this phenomenon. But is it the
real reason? Or is this phenomenon reflective of religious coexistence? She also
explains why people might mix.

People . . . . need to have a certain security, security of work, security from the
standpoint of health and the health of theirs, . . .security to be sure they will live
a long time because, . . . in Benin, one lives in an environment of fear of the
other. One always has the impression that the other is jealous, and . . . can be
after you at any moment. So there is this . . . fear which makes it so that there is
always a search for security . . . One looks for it in religion. Yes, it is traditional
religion, that is what I have said. There are no borders.

What does the respondent do when she is sick? This question did not seem appropriate for a physician but I asked anyway. Her response includes the expected—using modern medicine—but also the unexpected plant alternatives.

When I am sick I use the knowledge in my head . . . because I studied classical
medicine, but I have also practiced homeopathy, and I have done research in
medicinal plants, so . . . I am convinced that a physician must know more than
one thing, that is why I have become interested. . . . I am convinced that classical medicine is not affordable for the majority of my people because it is too
expensive and it is not accepted by the majority of the population. That is why I
have invested in researching alternatives to be able to help for the least cost to
my clients.

The mix of traditional medicine does not include sacrifices to divinities. In the
respondent's view, it is important that both pharmacopée and modern medicine
be used to ensure the successful outcome of treatment. This is an example of
inculturation. No aspect is incompatible with Catholicism. Earlier the respon-

dent provided another example of inculturation—the Revenant who goes to the house of the dead.

> Inculturation . . . is not traditional religion. It is the culture; what is good in the culture . . . and gives an answer . . . that is, where the baptized . . . can find himself, that's all. That is really to find himself and to say that, "that is mine." . . . Inculturation is a good thing.

More problems with inculturation.

If Catholic religious rites were inculturated "the Beninese would find himself." Another problem with inculturation, however, is the diversity of ethnic groups and the question of what to include from these cultures.

> The cultures are not the same. So when they are going to inculturate . . . the other does not find himself. Ethnic groups are very different. . . . From North to South, it is very different, and may be from East to West is also different. That is the colonial heritage. Yes, they have assembled ethnic groups that have nothing in common and the consequence is that, in the same country, there are a multitude of ethnic groups and multiplicity of languages. People do not understand each other, and it is French that allows us to communicate.

These statements show the complexity of inculturation. Interestingly, the French language, the language of colonizers creates unity in diversity. But often, as discussed before, one hears conversations in Fon-gbe with French words scattered throughout, and an occasional switch from one language to the other.

Ethnic groups are like different West African musical instruments that have made their way into Catholic churches. The instruments are comparable to languages, each with different vocabulary and grammatical structure.

> There are instruments that link the population but the rites are different from North to South. But what is good is that we are open, we are open enough, and when, for example, one takes the chorales . . . they do the rhythm and all the dances of all sections in the country.

The difficulty faced by inculturation due to multiple ethnic groups is further explained.

> Let's say . . . I am from one ethnic group, and you are from another, there are chorales that do not sing in the language of this ethnic group. There is never a mix, because the rhythms are not the same. But to the contrary, the chorale of the youth, as the young—are people who went to school, are educated and they mix all of it because they have tam- tam, guitars—they take the . . . other language of the country and . . . mix them. But the ethnic chorales do not mix because the rhythms are specific to each ethnic group. One can use the same tam tam. . . . [But] even if it is the same, the rhythm is never the same.

> One must inculturate without going beyond the essential in the Church. Some-
> thing has to be done to create a unicity. So what can create unicity in the
> Church? People coming from the outside must be able to find themselves at
> home, because it is the house of the Father, and he is in the house.

The young and educated bridge this gap between ethnic cultures. Education and
generation offer a solution to the problem of unifying diverse ethnic groups.
Education and generation can also solve the problems associated with inculturation.

It is important to be selective in what is inculturated. The respondent approves of limited inculturation. She also mentions the more trivial aspects of
inculturation, like wearing traditional outfits and preparing meals that are local
as important to transmit to future generations.

> Regarding meals too, I do put forward my maximum effort to prepare meals of
> the tradition so my children will discover traditional meals, and especially what
> we ate when we were little. I try to make them discover all that. . . . I do not
> have the time, I cannot do everything, but that is close to my heart.

Women who carry children on their backs while they play with them, work
with them, even dance with them, are the most likely transmitters of culture.
The same may be true regarding the transmission of an inculturated Catholic imagination. Here too, women especially educated women may be the
most likely transmitters..

Conclusion

The face of Catholicism in Benin does not lend itself to easy description. Voices
heard in this chapter suggest an interplay of tradition and modernity, a fluid hybridity ranging from double-belonging (Catholicism and system Vodou), to inculturation (Catholicism and intuitive Vodou). This hybridity is also evident in
the treatment of illnesses, which may or may not involve the system Vodou. As
will be evident in the next chapter, the family plays an important role in the religious choices people make in everyday life and ultimately outcomes for presentation of the sacramental self from double belonging to inculturation.

Chapter four
Pluralism and the extended family

> *La pression familiale est forte. . . . [I]ls sont*
> *tiraillés entre leur foi et la pression*
> *familiale. Ce qui fait qu'ils viennent*
> *chercher secours, l'assistance du prêtre qui*
> *a pour rôle de prier et de supporter ces*
> *fidèles. Ils viennent poser le problème. Le*
> *mélange vient de là, et pour remédier il faut*
> *une éducation doctrinale, une éducation . . .*
> *pour les enraciner dans la foi.*

In Benin, pluralism within the extended family accompanies religious pluralism. The family, where various types of religious unions coexist, is a microcosm of the society. One can speak of family unity within religious diversity. One could also speak of familial-interreligious networks. Like Aderanti Adepoju writes (1999: 90),

> La famille est le noyau d'une existence à la fois individuelle et communautaire, l'espace au sein duquel une personne fait l'expérience de la conscience personnelle, individuellement et en relation avec les autres membres de la société. Au sein d'une même famille ou d'un ménage, on peut relever la coexistence de deux mondes totalement différents: les enfants peuvent étudier á l'université tandis que leurs parents restent illéttrés et principalement occupés à cultiver leur champs avec de pauvres 'bâtons de bois'. Dans une telle famille, il y a deux éventails d'attentes, de niveaux économiques, de préoccupations culturelles et de visions du monde.

> (The family is the core of an existence simultaneously individual and communitarian, the space in which a person becomes conscious of a personal conscience, individually and in relation to the other members of the society. Within

the same family or of a household, one can see the coexistence of two completely different worlds: the children may study at the university while their
parents remain illiterate and mainly occupied cultivating their fields with the
poor 'sticks of wood'. In such a family are two fans [forms] of waiting, economic levels, cultural concerns and visions of the world).

Family life leads family members to accept two (or even more) religious
visions of the world. The family «exerce de fortes pressions 'sur les individus
qui la constituent, pressions qui peuvent apparaître irrationnelles mais qui en fait
sont fondées sur les traditions sociales'. . . . La famille maintient son emprise sur
les individus même dans les questions les plus intimes» (Adepoju 1999: 14, 24)
[The family "exerts strong pressures 'on the individuals who constitute it,
pressures which can appear irrational but in fact are founded on social
traditions.' . . . The family maintains its influence on individuals even in the
most intimate issues]. Intragenerational pressure to conform affects the collective intergenerational memory.

Why refer to the family in this work? Obedience to family traditions is an
important part of African normative system. Disobedience could lead to serious
consequences. Obedience is expected. As one scholar puts it, "'Le vrai ennemi
n'est pas ailleurs, il est dans la famille,' entend-on dire souvent" (Kinkpon,
2007) [The true enemy is not elsewhere, it is in the family,' is often heard]. It is
in this daily socio familial context that religious beliefs are practiced.

Beninese culture is so complex it would be pretentious to claim understanding it thoroughly or explaining it well. But at least the following is clear: it
is not possible to separate religious daily life from the extended family. Religion
and family form a dancing couple. The interviews show in the same family, that
one can find a Catholic priest whose brother is chief of traditional religion. Several cases are in the larger sample. Also, whether of nuclear or extended type,
inside the same family are Moslems, Catholics, Animists, Celestials, Protestant
(Evangelicals) and other denominations. In the event of difficulty or suffering, a
Catholic family member may seek help from non Catholic members. These are
interactions that family life facilitates with its traditional ceremonies in which
every member is expected to participate—whether Christian or not. A family
member, also member of the Celestial Church can propose to a sick relative who
is Catholic a visit of cure to the Celestial Church. Or, if this Celestial member
has the necessary formation to recite prayers and do the rituals, he himself may
do so. It would be similar for a family member who practices another religion
such as Vodou. If the patient is cured or suffering decreases, s/he attributes this
relief to the power of that religion now attractive to the beneficiary who may
become a follower or keep with this religion an intimate contact—an affection
developed from the good received.

Religious coming-and-going is supported and imposed by the family. Family cohesion encourages, even demands micro religious pluralism. The family
facilitates encounters and cohesion with other religions. Recall Adepoju: «La
famille est le noyau d'une existence à la fois individuelle et communautaire,

l'espace au sein duquel une personne fait l'expérience de la conscience personnelle, individuellement et en relation avec les autres membres de la société» [The family is the core of an existence» together communitarian, the space within which a person makes the experiment of personal conscience, individually and in relation to other members of the society].

Thus, the family is the vehicle which transmits tradition and encourages the coming-and-going between one kin and the other. It invites bricolage. But is this invitation to a bricolage of faith or culture? Is it a religious syncretism—a reinvented Catholic faith? A majority of respondents think that there is a mix of religion in Benin but, they say they, themselves, do not mix. It may be that what appears only mixture of religions has instead as its components Beninese culture and religious faith—an inculturated faith, where the adept recognizes himself in its practice whatever faith may be; it is a faith that has now become hers/his as it ceases to be simply "yovoed"[25] or "imported." As one priest-respondent explains:

Oui [les catholiques mélangent] . . . . Nos chrétiens sont des gens qui aiment beaucoup mélanger. Même en regardant les membres de ma famille on voit que le syncrétisme est un peu développé. C'est à dire que face aux problèmes de la vie, tout de suite la plupart de nos chrétiens catholiques sont ébranlés. Quand je dis les problèmes de la vie au Bénin [je parle de] . . . la maladie, la sorcellerie tout ce qui met le Chrétien mal à l'aise. Ca les pousse à revenir au niveau de la religion traditionnelle. Mais je pense qu'avec le temps ça va reculer puisque il y a beaucoup de groupes de prières aujourd'hui qui existent sur les paroisses pour porter et aider ces Chrétiens qui sont en difficulté. Parce que ne sachant pas à qui s'adresser—le prêtre lui dit la messe, il s'en va, on ne le voit pas—bon si ces groupes de prières comme le Renouveau . . . si ce Chrétien fait parti de l'un de ces groupes il sait qu'il est pris en charge par ce groupe ce qui évite vraiment la dispersion, le syncrétisme. Mais je reconnais en même temps que au niveau de la famille—je reviens toujours au niveau de la famille—la pression familiale est forte à vous amener à utiliser, à pratiquer le syncrétisme parce que je . . . parle même ma petite expérience, j'ai béni plusieurs mariages et récemment il y a un couple dont j'ai célébré le mariage. Ils ont des problèmes pour avoir d'enfants. Quand la femme tombe enceinte, il y a des malaises, des phénomènes. . . . De l'autre coté, la famille leur propose qu'ils aillent consulter certaines personnes . . . donc ils sont tiraillés entre leur foi et la pression familiale. Ce qui fait qu'ils viennent chercher secours, l'assistance du prêtre qui a pour rôle de prier et de supporter ces fidèles. Ils viennent poser le problème. Le mélange vient de là, et pour remédier il faut une éducation doctrinale, une éducation . . . pour les enraciner dans la foi.

Yes [Catholics mix]. . . . Our Christians are people like to mix. Even looking at the members of my own family one sees that syncretism is developed. That in the face of life's problems, immediately the majority of Catholic Christians is shaken. In Benin, when I say problems of the life to Benin [I am referring to] . . . disease, sorcery, all that does not put a Christian at ease. This is what pushes them toward traditional religion. But I think that this will change since there are many groups of prayers today in parishes to help Christians facing difficulty.

> Because there is nowhere to turn—the priest says Mass and goes away, one does not see him—it is good to have groups of prayers as the Revival. . . . [I]f this Christian belongs to one of these groups, s/he knows that it is dealt with by this group what avoids really dispersion, the syncretism. But I recognize at the same time at the level of the family—I always return to the level of the family—family pressure is strong and leads you to practice syncretism because I . . . speak even of my small experiment, I have blessed several marriages and recently there is a couple whose marriage I celebrated. They have problems having children. When the woman becomes pregnant, there is fainting and other phenomena. On the other hand, the family proposes to them that they consult certain people... they are pulled between faith and the family pressure. With the result that they come to seek help. They seek the assistance of a priest whose role is to support them. They come to pose the problem. Religious mixture comes from here and, for a cure, there needs to be doctrinal education, an education . . . to ground them in the faith.

The influence of the family is clear in this testimony deserving of deeper analysis. The couple wants to obey due to respect for the extended family, traditions and normative expectations of the society. But even as they do so, also wish to hold on to their achieved faith. This thought-provoking statement suggests for the couple a concern with preserving the collective memory of the family but also concern with the forced syncretism that may ensue from pressures to conform. Religious pluralism within families can be a source of tensions. Borders appear fluid yet are informally monitored and negotiated on an on-going basis.

In West Africa's everyday life, religious faiths interact. One faith influences the other just as Islam impacts Animism and vice versa (Parrinder: 1959: 141).

> If animism influences Islam in West Africa, and gives it characteristics of its own, it is just as true that Islam affects animism. Muslim traders are notorious vendors of amulets, in which a verse from the Qur'an may replace the magical leaves of the pagan amulet. Because of the tolerance and syncretism of animism, Muslim teaching and mythology find easy entrance into pagan myth. Muslim ritual (naming, circumcision, marriage, etc.) may easily fit in with traditional practice (Parrinder, 1959: 140).

In sum, religious behavior does not occur in isolation. As Islam impacts traditional religion especially in the Northern Region, Catholicism in the South could have an impact on the Celestial Church, the Evangelical Church, Islam, traditional religion, and vice versa to the extent that these coexist in society and the family. It is like a dynamic multiple-lane street with blurred, almost imperceptible dividing lines. It can also be represented by softly colliding vehicles each carrying surface marks of the other, but holding even deeper marks of the ancestral tradition. It is a system supported by the family subsystem.

Possible Outcomes of Religious Interaction

A multiple way street or contact do not mean the original structure or traditional identity lost. Nor does religious mixing mean a complete loss of faith in one's own tradition. In the following quote, author Catherine Cornille (2003: 45) illustrates this idea by offering the example of Buddhism and Christianity:

> A Christian may identify with some aspects of the Buddhist analysis of suffering and may adopt some of the Buddhist techniques for overcoming suffering without fundamentally challenging his own commitment to Christianity. . . . However, this selective adoption of beliefs and practices of a different religious tradition does not constitute double belonging (Cornille, 2003: 45).

When parts of another religion thought to fit one's own are selected for inclusion, the concept "double belonging" does not apply since one has simply selected from the other religion those aspects that are compatible with it. It is not "double belonging" because there is no real change in the original belief or practice. One cannot even speak of an added element, since what is included either fills a preexisting space or comfortably carves its own space. There is no incompatibility between pre-existing and adopted elements. Though the forms may be different, the essentials remain. Said differently, there is either no difference, or whatever difference makes no real difference. Everything either fits, or seems to fit. So what is double belonging?

> [T]he loss of one's original or primary religious commitment may also lead to a genuinely intermediate position in which one tradition is normative in certain areas of belief and practice and another tradition in other areas. . . . It is here that one might rightly speak of an experience of double religious belonging. . . a form of syncretism (Cornille, 2003: 46).

In the case of double belonging, there may be two or more different teachers—one from each practice adopted.

> The question of the possibility of double belonging presents itself when confronted with the totality of religious beliefs and practices, whereupon the encounter with conflicting or incompatible claims to absolute truth becomes unavoidable (Cornille, 2003: 45).

"Conflict" and "incompatible" are key words in double belonging. In the *Souls of Black Folk*, W.E.B. Du Bois describes the double consciousness of the "Negro" torn between, and attempting to reconcile, two identities—African and American. Double consciousness fits the definition of double belonging and idea of incompatibility.

The similarities between syncretism and double belonging are clear. In both cases, the elements brought together are not compatible resulting in the faithful moving from one constituent to the other. It is like having "each foot in two different worlds." It is a coming and going between two planets, coming and going that creates confusion. As one scholar-respondent puts it, syncretism is like doing "la navette entre Dieu et le fétiche" [going back and forth between God to the fetish]. Syncretism or double belonging are also like living simultaneously in two different social structures or "serving two masters simultaneously," each with incompatible demands. The existence of conflict, or the potential for it, separates these two concepts—syncretism and double belonging—from bricolage, another outcome of religious interaction.

I use bricolage in the sense of a self-made, individualistic religion, result of religious encounter (Cornille, 2003: 46). Bricolage means a newly adopted religious element does not conflict (is not incompatible) with the original faith but a "collage" of something that previously did not exist in the original faith. I also think of bricolage as the removal of certain elements from a particular tradition without discarding the original identity. Coming to mind is a similar term, sometimes used to describe American Catholics who "pick and choose" what they like from their practice, while leaving out that with which they disagree or dislike. "Cafeteria Catholic" is that term. Cafeteria Catholics construct their own version of Catholicism as they pick and choose from Church teachings and practice what they prefer. Such Catholics are engaged in a bricolage. One example of what they leave out might be confession, an increasingly rare practice in the United States. Another is in the Catholic widespread use of artificial means of birth control. By picking and choosing what they like and leaving out what they do not like, Cafeteria Catholics have constructed their own version of Catholicism.

The bricolage concept can be extended to those who chose from the compatible one aspect here, and another there, remove this or that from here, mix it with that there, but still identify primarily with one religion to which they are attached and have constructed in their own way. This is not double belonging because there is no conflict or incompatibility with the existing practice. It is a case of religious reconstruction with compatible blocks that did not exist in the original version. Elements perceived essential or nonessential are "added" to or removed from this original in creative ways. Bricolage is innovative and different from double belonging. Bricolage is appendage. Though an addition as double belonging, it is fitting one and may go unnoticed. Double belonging and syncretism may cause clash, strain, conflict or incompatibility. "In spite of attempts to rid this term [syncretism] of pejorative meanings, it still denotes the (illegitimate) mixing of irreconcilable truths" (Cornille, 2003: 46).

Syncretism and double belonging do not last forever. They are transitory and part of an on-going process of cultural (religious) change. Eventually, these elements may fuse, or assimilate progressively into the existing practice. Clearly compatible from the start, the bricolage is an easier and quicker fit. And so is inculturation, a close relative.

What is inculturation.

Sometimes, in the scholarly literature, double belonging is termed inculturation—buzz concept in West African Catholic theology. But what exactly is inculturation? Is it the same as double belonging and syncretism? And is there a useful sociological concept that might be synonymous with it?

> [T]he attempt to reformulate one religious tradition through the worldview of philosophical framework of another . . . is often called the process of 'inculturation.' . . . [V]irtually every religious tradition must face the problem of the adaptation of a religious tradition to a cultural context different from the one where it first presents itself (Cornille 2003: 46).

West Africans had, still have to adapt their religious traditions to Christian contexts. Indeed, much literature on inculturation is found among Catholic theologians of West Africa. Here, I am thinking particularly of such scholars and theologians as Abbé Barthélemy Adoukonou, and other members of *Sillon Noir*.[26] Founded in Benin in 1970 by Adoukonou, the movement is also called *Méwihwendo*. Sillon Noir

> s'est donné pour but la redécouverte et la relecture chrétienne de la culture africaine dans toutes ses dimensions. L'apport spécifique de ce mouvement est la prise en compte du caractère oral de cette culture. Seuls des « intellectuels communautaires » chrétiens pourront produire une théologie africaine et purifier la culture traditionnelle en la faisant passer par la Croix.[27]

> has had as its goal the rediscovery and Christian rereading of African culture in all its dimensions. The specific contribution of this movement is the taking into account the oral character of that culture. Only Christian "communitarian intellectuals" [public intellectuals] will be able to produce an African theology and purify the traditional culture by making pass through the Cross.]

Members of Sillon Noir hope to inculturate West African Catholicism which involves much more than language. Indeed "[t]o attempt to reformulate a religion in categories and symbols belonging to a different cultural context implies engagement with the religion or religions that traditionally have shaped that culture"(Cornille, 2003: 47).

There appears engagement between Catholicism and traditional religion in Benin. Traditional or ancestral religion—Vodou—shaped Beninese culture. But the Sillon Noir is very careful how it engages traditional religion, and what from this traditional it includes in Catholic rituals. Members of this group study traditional rites carefully before their inclusion. The goal is to inculturate and to engage in Catholicism (imported religion) what in the traditional culture of West Africa does not conflict but is compatible with it.

[Engagement] may occur on a superficial level, through the adoption of external symbols. . . . Or it may take place on a deeper level, through the radical reformulation of one religion according to the worldview and philosophical categories of another. It is on this latter level that the question of double belonging
appears (Cornille, 2003: 46-47).

"Superficial" engagement (inculturation) through external symbols of clothing is
most visible, even though here too, and especially in cosmopolitan Cotonou,
there are many signs of globalization and modernity. For example, jeans have
made their appearance and become more and more popular. Though still uncommon, hair is straightened. It appears light skin does not yet have the meaning that it acquired in the Western Hemisphere, but stores do carry skin lighten-
ers. However, this is not yet a trend. What is more trendy and obvious are signs
of "reverse inculturation"—Americans, Europeans and other tourists adopting
the external symbols and ways of locals. Whether European American, African
Americans, or European, many choose African clothing with braided hair. One
hears foreigners speak a little or a lot of fon-gbe here and there. These visitors
say they are and do seem, thrilled to be there.

During Catholic celebrations, the most popular forms of dress are African.
Most men wear *boubous* in the most preferred color white (also traditional color
of Vodou). On special occasions, women have their heads wrapped in elegant
atchoke with matching outfits made of pagne cloth (African fabric). Here too,
white seems preferred. Other forms of inculturation considered superficial are
large, colorful umbrellas traditionally for kings, visible over the Holy Sacrament
during religious processions and at other times. Inside churches are the *tata
somba* shaped repositories; chairs similar in design to those used by kings;
priest's chasuble and altar coverings also in pagne cloth; West African instruments such as the popular drum, gong, bell and rattle to name only a few; old
and young in traditional outfit dancing and clapping in front of the Holy Sacrament. These are only some examples of inculturation considered more superficial that give a Beninese context to the practice of Catholicism.

On a more substantive level, signs of inculturation are obvious in attempts
to reformulate aspects of Catholicism. These are more controversial than the
earlier mentioned. Without being prompted, most respondents describe funeral
rites as best example of substantive inculturation. Upon the death of a relative,
each family offers a pagne later divided into three pieces. As reported by respondents, one piece is placed in the coffin, one piece given to the poor, and
another piece kept by the family. Though some respondents approve of these
rites, most others do not. This form of inculturation is particularly critiqued by
some Vodou priests and adepts who think the manner in which these final rites
are inculturated leaves out their most important symbolic aspects. In the views
of these priests, taking parts of a religious practice here and there yields superficial results only because the pieces and symbols lose their original meaning,
their holistic character and links to a particular set of beliefs and deities.

Inculturation is not double belonging or syncretism. Inculturation is more like a bricolage, though at a different level. The concept inculturation is used primarily in theological studies, but I find it useful here and quite similar to "ethnogenesis" the sociological framework from the Race and Ethnicity that is applied to this study.

"[W]hat drives . . . [inculturation] is the wish to enlarge and enrich a tradition through its reformulation in different categories of interpretation" (Cornille, 2004: 4). And that is precisely what Sillon Noir attempts with Catholicism and traditional West African religion—"to enlarge and enrich a tradition." The Sillon Noir movement seeks to make people feel at home with Catholicism seen by many as foreign—some say imported, a religion "venue d'ailleurs" [coming from elsewhere]; a *yovo* religion.

Inculturation may be re-defined as the inclusion of oneself with one's culture into another culture, or perhaps adding to a foreign culture the compatible elements of one's own. Inculturation, a refined adaptation of old to new (or new to old) religious elements, may follow double belonging. "Those engaged in the aforementioned forms of inculturation probably do not view themselves as belonging to more than one religion" (Cornille, 2004: 47). Since the beliefs inculturated are compatible, the adepts do not see them as having been combined, but instead may consider new elements aspects of their original beliefs and/or practices shared with the other practice. Cornille's conclusion (2003: 48) is a critique of double belonging.

> Religion and religious belonging is about the complete surrender of one's own will and judgment to a truth and power that lies beyond or beneath one's own rational and personal judgment. While it is possible to engage with and to be enriched by encounters with other religious traditions, a truly religious attitude presupposes a norm beyond oneself from which, in the final account, the truth of the other religion is assessed.

This critique suggests double belonging is no belonging. It is a back and forth movement. It is a coming-and-going, a lack or total absence of conviction. In this case, religious identity is split and while some may disagree, split identity is no identity. Double belonging lacks the "surrender" to a unique religious power outside of oneself and the suppression of "believer's"judgement to it. "Double or multiple religious belonging always implies a certain holding back, . . or an inability to let go of one religion when in heart and mind one has already converted to another" (Cornille, 2003: 49).

The previous statement contains several important ideas but one that struck me most is the difficulty for some believers to let go of their original religion when they convert to another—an example of double belonging. This is not inculturation. A situation that might lead to double belonging is that of a man I interviewed in the Midwest, a cradle Catholic who converted to Methodism upon marrying his Methodist wife. He shared with me how he missed his original faith and practice. If this respondent decided to come-and-go between old and new practices, though we are dealing with two Christian faiths, his coming and going would represent double belonging.

Double belonging may be obvious in persons who have recently converted from one religion to another as in the previous example. But it may be more obvious in conversions from traditional West African religion to Catholicism, though such converts may be the ones to completely sever any kind of association with their original religion as in the case of most Evangelical and Muslim interviewees in Benin.

Inculturation is different. Native Americans in the United States provide another good example.

> Native communities have long woven the stories, signs, and practices of the Christian tradition into the fabric of their lifeways, in rich and resourceful ways, even under the direst of colonizing circumstances. . . . Existing language in the scholarship on American religious history and Native American religious traditions as yet offers little guidance in making sense of the hybridity (McNally, 2000: 843).

When stories, signs and practices can be weaved, there appears no conflict between weaved elements. Rather than syncretism or double belonging, weaving as in Native American communities would be one form of inculturation. Yet, in the literature, weaving is usually presented as syncretism, leading to conceptual confusion. Thus, the call for a new framework that will make better sense of this form of hybridity.

> We . . . stand in need of an interpretive shift away from missionary intentions to some other paradigm that can better appreciate the finer workings of religion and culture. The signs and practices of the Christian tradition, variously presented by various Euro-American Christians to various native communities . . . especially the practices—became a medium through which many native people exercised their own agency . . . and through which some articulated resistance as well as accommodation (McNally 2000: 843).

In the case of Native Americans, the weaving of stories and signs with practices was not forced, but a natural process that may be termed inculturation. And the ethnogenesis perspective is one interpretive shift applicable to Native American religious hybridity. Ethnogenesis is also a fitting frame for West Africa. In this view, syncretism (or double belonging) and inculturation are segments on a continuum of increasing religio-cultural development. This study suggests ethnogenesis to be an appropriate framework for the study of religio-cultural contact and pluralism in West Africa.

Ethnogenesis

When two cultures come into contact there are a number of possible outcomes (Feagin and Feagin, 1999). The ethnogenesis framework in race and ethnic relations suggests one outcome to be the rise of ethnicity (from the Greek ethnos=people, folk, race; and genesis=birth).

At the point of original contact, native and nonnative cultures share one or more elements, language most often. In due time however, with exposure to education and the passing of generations, there is a give and take between incoming and host cultures. A process of cultural exchange and change becomes evident in the birth and progressive rise of ethnicity. While some of the original native and nonnative cultures remain intact, overtime intact areas decrease, while areas shared increase. The native culture partially integrates nonnative elements, resulting in a new, progressively redefined identity.[28]

How then might the ethnogenesis framework apply to colonization and religions in Benin and West Africa? At the point of contact, colonizers (nonnative) and colonized (natives) shared neither language nor religion. But they shared beliefs in a Supreme Being, a monotheistic religion (Alladaye, 2003: 31), an afterlife, even though the names they used for this Being and their conceptions of monotheism and afterlife differed widely. Colonizers called this Being God. Native Africans in the South of Benin who believed in spirit life called it Mawu (or Mawu-Lisa). While there was not only one but several traditional religions, all were ancestral and, in this way, closer to one another in terms of beliefs and practices than they were to the imported religions (Alladaye, 2003: 25, 26). African natives and non natives also differed from non natives in their ideas on how to reach this Supreme or Spirit Being. For natives, Mawu was accessible through a pantheon of lesser gods or divinities. Legba stands between Mawu and divinities and facilitates communication between them. A representation of Legba is in front of many homes because he is considered guardian and protector of families. "Legba n'est pas une divinité qui fait du mal. Il protège la maison. C'est le guerrier qui défend la maison quand les maltraiteurs vont venir. Ce n'est pas le diable. Le diable est un malfaiteur" (Alladaye, 2003 : 29). [Legba is not a divinity that hurts. Legba protects the house. It is the warrior who defends the house when bad people are going to come. It is not the devil. The devil is a bad person]. Because Mawu was abstraction, she had to be represented. Here is an example of the invisible in the visible.

Yet despite religious abstractions, when asked about their own visions of the afterlife and what they think might happen then (or there), most respondents adept of Vodou respond: "who has been there and come back? No one has ever been there and come back." It is safe to assume the respondents apparent focus on the concrete—what can be seen, smelled, heard, touched, felt, the earthy—is also part of West African natives' historical tradition. But this concrete is also combined with abstraction. In his excellent study of Catholics in Benin, Alladaye maintains, when adepts of Vodun are praying in front of pieces of wood, or "mottes de terre" [mounts of earth], or pieces of iron, (the earthy) it is not these specific "things" (wood, earth and iron) that they are adoring. Adoration goes beyond these pieces of material culture. Objects, including "mottes de terre" pieces of wood, iron, and others are only symbols. They stand for the invisible. They are representations of the abstract that make it much easier for the mind to center on that abstract. These concrete, material "things" are vehicles to the nonmaterial for anyone but in an oral culture they take on added importance. They are the unwritten writing. They help read and explain the abstract. They link concrete and abstract. They operationalize that abstract. It is much like a picture or tattoo representing someone dear who passed away serves to remember that person. A picture works as a symbol of his/her spiritual presence. A picture helps the individual retain individual and collective memories.

Of course there is always the risk that representations might lead to superstition, as the objects themselves become targets of adoration. Chances of this occurring might be much higher again in a context where rates of literacy are low. However, this risk of superstition could also happen with statues in Catholic churches or similar religious contexts where in the minds of believers, the representative object become confused with what it represents (see Greeley, 2000).

Additionally, it is also important to recognize that representative "things" in traditional religion are not automatically sacred. It is not any motte de terre, piece of iron, piece of wood, or any other object that is worth adoration.

Dans la société dahoméenne traditionnelle, ce n'était jamais chaque plante, chaque morceau de fer qui faisaient l'objet d'une vénération des populations. Elle ne rendait culte qu'à travers des objets ayant reçu une sanctification particulière de la part des personnes habituées à la conférer et dans les conditions requises (Alladaye, 2003: 28).

[In Dahomean traditional society, it is not each plant, each piece of iron that was the object of veneration of populations. The object of cult was through objects having received a special sanctification from people used to confer it and within the required conditions].

Like missionaries praying in front a cross, West Africans had the capacity to abstract and were not engaging simply in what erroneously has been named fetischism (see Alladaye, 2003).

I am not an initiate of Vodou, thus what follows may be due to my own lack of insights into this complex ancestral religion but to me, this difference sounds much like that found between a statue, cross, water, or rosary that have been blessed (has received "special sanctification from people used to confer it") and a statue, cross, water, or rosary that have not. When blessed, such objects are transformed spiritually and take believers closer yet to what they represent. These objects go from being simple representations to being sacramentals.

These representations are similarities Dahomeans and missionaries shared at the first point of contact. "Sanctified objects" of traditional religion's "sacramentals." These found their Catholic equivalent in blessed candles, blessed water, blessed rosaries, and others. But besides these similarities, or "almost similarities" some might argue, the two populations differed in how to get access to the Supreme Being. For traditionalist, Mawu was far and accessible only through deities.

Besides differing conceptions of Dahomeans and missionaries regarding the Supreme Being and afterlife there were also differences in their practice of their religion. According to Alladaye, in traditional religion, there was

absence de prosélytisme à base de respect mutuel pour la croyance des autres. . . . Le contraste est en effet saisissant entre cette acceptation de la différence dans le culte vodun et la ferme volonté du christianisme de n'admettre d'autre 'vérité' religieuse que la sienne propre» (Alladaye, 2003 : 38)

[absent proselytism based upon mutual respect for the beliefs of others . . . The contrast is in fact shocking between this acceptance of difference in the Vodun cult and the firm will of Christianity to admit no other religious "truth" than its own].

This highlights the importance of respect for and openness to the other in traditional religion. But the lack of proselytism could also be due to a consensus among Dahomeans, that for whatever reasons missionaries were incapable of being proselytized. Absent proselytism could also be due to natives having regarded traditional (ancestral) religions so webbed to their own culture, physical presence, appearance, way of life, they did not even consider the possibility that others so different might fit in—others meaning yovo Europeans especially. Missionaries were not recognizable for they neither look, spoke, or acted like ancestors. Indeed, this second proposition seems supported also by Alladaye when he writes,

Le culte vodun plonge ses racines dans la conception du monde chez les populations du pays, dans leur degré d'évolution technique et dans leur compréhension des rapports sociaux. Il en résulte chez elles un profond attachement aux valeurs et aux capacités réelles ou supposées de cette religion. . . . Tel était le milieux socio-religieux dans lequel s'inscrivit l'action missionnaire Catholique (Alladaye, 2003: 39).

[The Vodun cult dips its roots in the conception of the world of the populations of the country, in their degree of technical evolution and in their understanding of social relations. The result here is a profound attachment to the values and capacities real or supposed of this religion. . . . Thus was the socio-religious milieu in which was inscribed the Catholic missionary action].

The Vodun religion was an expression of a particular society—Dahomean society. Natives were not ready for the implantation of a new religion, one that, at the time did not fit their social structure. To them this imported Christian religion was *yovo*. It was "une religion venue d'ailleurs." Missionaries appear to have imagined differently the relationship between Supreme Being and society. Dahomeans were closer to Durkheim's view of God as society.

Colonizers (also yovo) presented themselves as Christians. Missionaries, appearing for the first time around 1860—many considered supporters of colonizers—were met with skepticism. As Alladaye explains, there are many reasons for this resistance, including a sense that the existing social order which included strict obedience to royalty was being undermined. Not only was there a local structure in place that was to be protected, but there was also value consensus that held together the society. Such values as cooperation, solidarity were important to the social order and had to be preserved. There were specific norms that derived from these values. These norms applied to the general population. Everyone including the king was expected to abide. Consensus and normative order meant stability, predictability. Religious conversion to Christianity would reflect an individualism not compatible with the existing communitarian character of the social structure. Religion was one major component of that structure (Alladaye, 2003, 16, 19-20).

The practice of Catholicism, or any Christian religion for that matter, was not an option at the time (Alladaye, 2003). Dahomean society was sacred space. Distancing from this space was distancing from the tradition, the social structure—in sum, the normative expectations. Distancing would likely carry severe consequences. One could lose the blessings of ancestors. It is like encountering fierce resistance upon forcing oneself with one's values into someone's sacred home space.

Traditional religion is ancestral and handed down to generation after generation by forefathers. The communitarian character of traditional religion and its focus on sharing is expressed in this common dictum: "un homme ne doit pas rester à l'ombre quand son frère est au soleil" (Hazoumé 1937: 36 as cited in Alladaye, 2003: 24). [a man must not stay in the shade when his brother is in the sun]. This was an African value, part of the sacred space not to be violated. Young Africans were taught these values. They were to honor and serve their ancestors, show respect for elders and practice community (Alladaye 2003). Solidarity and community were part of the cultural and religious traditions. The values of imported religions that stressed singularity deviated from this consensus. These deviations make clear why Christianity did not flourish immediately in Benin (Alladaye, 2003). To depart from native ancestral traditions would mean departure from sacred traditions. In sum, "Malgré la diversité des peuples du Dahomey, il existait avant l'introduction du Christianisme, une certaine unité spirituelle traditionnelle reposant sur le culte des ancêtres" (Alladaye, 2003:38). [Despite the diversity of the people of Dahomey, there existed before the introduction of Christianity a certain traditional spiritual unity resting on the cult of ancestors.]

This sense of solidarity and community which characterized the old society continues today despite the evidence of modernity. The family includes not only members that are alive but also the dead. Family unity and solidarity is expressed for example in the warm hospitality extended not only to members of one's family but also strangers. In Benin, visitors drop in unannounced and, if this visit is during meals, whatever is served to the family is also served to the guest made welcome. The guest accepts the offer without any apology for the unexpected visit. It is business as usual. It is culture alive. Not extending hospitality to this visitor is what might require an apology.

Other expressions of solidarity are evidenced in fictive kinship. In Benin, when someone refers to someone else as their brother or their sister (I seldom heard the word "cousin" which, apparently, has a negative connotation) it does not necessarily mean their biological brother or sister. I learned this during my first year visit. So when someone was introduced to me as brother or sister, I learned to ask "how is he your brother?" "How is she your sister?" Then, I would find out they are considered a brother or sister because coming from the same village. Especially being from the same village qualifies one as brother or sister. The village is an extended family.

But someone from outside the village also may be considered a brother or sister. People of the African diaspora are brothers and sisters. Fictive kinship fits the social structure, the idea of an extended community and solidarity. The world is the largest extended family, explaining the warm hospitable behaviors offered strangers. Hospitality to strangers is important—a stranger that might have been sent by ancestors or may be an ancestor in disguise. Here again prevails the idea of family, the importance of blessings from ancestors, doing as the ancestors want or would have wanted. Early on, these values perceived irreconcilable differences with Christian missionary culture led to native resistance to their teachings.

Père Aupiais and Inculturation.

Bolaji Idowu (1973: 86) writes,

> There came the time when there were missionaries who began to feel that a knowledge of the Africans from inside was necessary for the success of their work of evangelism—for how can you speak to a person whom you do not understand and who does not understand you?

In the 20th century resistance to Christianity began to lessen. Père Aupiais deserves special mention, not only because he is so recognized by the Beninese but also his contribution to inculturation in Benin. Père Aupiais contextualized his message and to evangelize,

> composa le livret d'une sorte de drame sacré rappelant les Mystères du Moyen-Age, le "Mystère de l'Épiphanie" où les Rois Mages, devenus les chefs du peuple Gun, qui venaient à la crèche adorer le "vrai Dieu" et lui consacrer leur pays et leur sujets. Les acteurs étaient Gun, la langue était le gun, les coutumes

étaient la reproduction du protocole en honneur à la cour des rois gun, la musique des chants était celle employée durant les cérémonies et les danses qui accompagnaient l'élection et le couronnement du roi (Alladaye 2003: 147-148)

[composed a sort of sacred drama about the Mysteries of the Middle Ages, the Mystery of the Epiphany where the kings who had become chiefs of Gun people, were coming to the manger to adore the real God and consecrate their country and subjects to Him. The actors were Gun, the language was gun, the customs reproduced the protocol of gun kings, the music of chants was that used during ceremonies and dances that accompanied the election and the crowning of the king].

Other innovations also borrowed from local culture to successfully package Christian ideas. La *Fête des Mariages* is another example.

[L]'institution de la 'Fête des Mariages' en 1925. Ce n'était rien moins qu'une grande fête paroissiale, organisée pour la régularisation d'unions illégitimes. Dans un pays «chrétien» une pareille fête eut fait scandale et eut semblé une prime à l''inconduite'. Dans un pays comme le Dahomey où le nombre de chrétiens polygames était élevé et celui des femmes chrétiennes très réduit et où bien d'autres obstacles encore s'opposaient au mariage chrétien et à la persévérance dans le respect de ses lois, le P. Aupiais pensa qu'il convenait au contraire, d'accueillir avec des démonstrations de joie les pauvres chrétiens qui avaient le courage de se réconcilier avec Dieu et avec la 'Morale chrétienne.' (Alladaye, 2003: 148).

[T]he institution of the 'Feast of Marriages'in 1925. It was nothing more than a big parish celebration, organized to regulate illegitimate unions. In a 'Christian' country such a celebration would be scandalous and perceived an invitation to immoral behavior. In a country like Dahomey where the number of polygamous Christians was high and Christian women very low, and where other obstacles were contrary to Christian marriage and respect for its laws, the P. Aupiais thought that it was more appropriate to welcome with demonstrations of joy the poor Christians who had the courage to reconcile with God and 'Christian Morality.' The method could not lack giving greater trust to the parishioners of P. Aupiais and to attract their regard and their gratitude, all that was important to the success of missionary action].

These innovations were successful. And though the idea was to move natives to his side—a goal that may be perceived ethnocentric—such inventive mechanisms show Père Aupiais' respect for local culture.

What did Père Aupiais do differently? He was aware of cross-cultural differences between missionaries and locals. In his dealings with the Dahomeans, he engaged in cultural relativism. He met them where they were for he understood that there was an existing structure. He used the people's own transportation (culture) to lead them to his destination (evangelization). His method seems to have worked.

Today, after generations of yovo education and the result of continued infusion in the neo-colonial society, the official language is the language of colonizers. Moreover, today, whether of Catholic or traditional religious affiliation, most decision makers have a catholic education. My interviews with Vodou priests revealed many attended Catholic elementary schools and received an education about which they speak positively. It is in these schools that they received the sacraments of the Catholic Church (for most, except marriage). Currently, many have children attending Catholic schools and see no conflict between the two sets of values. This appreciation for Catholic education is evident in the words of a high dignitary of traditional religion in the opening chapter, "I would like to have schools for the Vodou religion that use the same principle as Catholic schools because Catholic schools are so good and so successful."[29]

[Ah, Catholic schools are a good thing. My wish now . . . I would like (and it is a message that I have to add to your question) we would like also that this school be also created at the level of our tradition so that our new adepts who are coming out of the convent go to school, so that tomorrow we may have professionals in our convents, because if missionaries, or Muslims, had not created their schools, we would not have professionals. Many professionals in this country have passed through there. That is why, we . . . our wish, my big "chantier," it is that I must do everything and I will do everything, I am going to pray so that the school of adepts sees the light. So, you have posed the question well, if the schools of missionaries are a good thing. We too would like that the schools of Vodou sees the day].

But as of today, the wish of this dignitary is not yet reality. The reality is still Catholic education moving and shaping a progressively more and more inculturated ethnic identity. If and when schools for Vodou adepts see the light, it is likely that the ethnogenesis would develop in a different direction, move more slowly in the same direction. This push for Vodou schools seems associated with a general sense among adepts that there is a need for the "revalorization of traditional religion." As one respondent put it:

On m'appelle Daah . . . Je suis un roi spirituel . . . Nous avons notre siège à [inaudible] à la région d' Abomey, département du Sud [pour la revalorisation du Culte Vodou]. . . . Donc c'est en vue de ce qui se passe avec les religions évangéliques . . . les religions évangéliques ça veut dire les religions importées au Bénin et compte tenu du dégât que ça pose sur le terrain que nous, nous sommes un groupe de responsable du culte, nous nous sommes entendus pour réparer notre culture traditionnelle. Puisque nous avons senti que l'envahisseur [inaudible] de sorte que notre culture traditionnelle [inaudible]. Donc ce groupe [inaudible] un pays qui pert sa tradition pert sa racine. . . . Et tout ce qui est évangélique ça veut dire est importée.

[So it is because of what is going on with the Evangelical religions . . . the Evangelical religions are the imported religions to Benin and given the trouble that they pose on this terrain we are a group of responsible for cults, we have

agreed to repair our traditional culture. This is because we feel the invader . . . .
our traditional culture. . . . A country which loses its tradition loses its roots. . . .
Everything evangelical is imported].

   It is unfortunate that the tape associated with this important interview was
damaged in travel so that the remainder cannot be shared. As for all other respondents, identifiers are removed even as the respondent asked to be identified.
I do so because there is no written permission. The necessity of which he speaks
may include traditional education—a return to respect, honor and worship for
the traditional cult, solidarity and cooperation. And if this were to happen it
would not only renew the traditional cult but also impact the direction of ethnogenesis.

   Vodou education is still in the future. Over several generations French
Catholic education—education which continues today—a cultural exchange
took place that led to the rise of a culture different from the original native,
though much of it persists. The respondent wants a return to cultural roots and
accuses imported religions, mostly Evangelical sects, of invading, dominating
and posing a threat to traditional culture.

   Outside the realm of religion, signs of ethnogenesis can be observed in the
mix of French with Fon-gbe, a dialect most commonly spoken in the Southern
region of Benin. Beninese southerners speaking Fong-be are often heard switch-
ing to French. There may be a French word here another French word there, a
sentence in fon-gbe here followed by a sentence or partial sentence in French
there. But it should be noted that French concepts are used to express what already exists in the culture, or has just come to exist but cannot yet be expressed
in the dialect.

   Also indicative of ethnogenesis outside of religion are manners of eating in
certain groups and settings. Whenever I went to an "ex-pat" restaurant, alone or
with colleagues and/or friends, I ate with a fork, and so did they. There was also
a fork which I used when invited to a home for lunch or dinner. In these settings,
even what the Beninese call "pate"or "fufu" such as *igname pilé*, requires utensils used in the West.

   Just before I left Benin, two colleagues from the University of Abomey-
Calavi took me to a restaurant in Porto Novo—a local restaurant where no forks,
knives or spoons were to be found on the table. Before our meal—which included fish, *amiyo*, a green leafy vegetable sauce whose name I do not remember, except it had the consistency of cooked okra—we were offered a bucket a
water to wash our hands in preparation for table work. This was my very first
experience in Benin (or anywhere else) eating a main meal with bare hands. As
my colleagues and I ate (with our hands), they commented on this Beninese tradition. I will admit, I enjoyed the experience so that I wondered why I had not
done this earlier. The food seemed to taste much better.

   Eating ustensils are one form of inculturation. Depending upon the context,
the Beninese use these utensils or their hands. I thought this comparable to native Hawaians who during family "luaus" will eat their poï and lomi lomi

salmon using the fingers (one-finger poï, two finger poï), but depending upon the context, may also use the fork. Here too, eating poï with a fork would be a form of inculturation, and evidence a superficial level of ethnogenesis.

Often, the "yovo" and traditional are found coexisting, though some statistics are firm in suggesting a percentage of the population remaining traditionalist especially outside of the urban areas. Of course, the religious situation is much too complex to rely on statistics. For obvious reasons, statistics (any statistics) about Benin or West Africa ought to be taken with a grain of salt. Here, as for other developing countries, data collection is not easy. Often, houses are not numbered and streets have no names. But even if these infrastructures were in place, it would still be difficult to get information from people not trusting strangers asking them personal questions. As soft-spokeness, discretion is a norm of Beninese culture. But let's say data collection could be done with ease: still, statistics would not measure hybridity well. Attempting to apply statistics in this case may be equivalent to showing approximately 12% of the American population black, without accounting for the mix in an heterogeneous society.

President Barack Obama is classified as African American or black even though sometimes jokingly he refers to himself as a "mutt." And a "mutt" he is. In the Haitian conception of race and ethnicity, he would be classified as "mulatto"—the offspring of black and white parents. But even as his European ancestry is discussed, pictures of his white grandparents and mother being shown, the media portrays him as African American and black. For the American media, the President is never black and white. He is never partially black. Perhaps this constructed identity reduces the complexity of double belonging and the idea of a double consciousness from a Du Boisian point of view troublesome for the African American imagination. But regardless of reasons, in data collection bi-racial types would no doubt skew that count. So it is with religious belonging in religiously "mutt" Benin. Biased too would numbers be that claim to accurately count religious belonging. Estimating the percentage of adepts of each religion, and painting an accurate picture of religious ethnogenesis at the micro level, if possible, would be most difficult.

Especially in villages where literacy is low, double belonging may be found. And it is here, in these villages, that incompatible parts of the original culture and religion would meet and potentially give rise to confusion. In the villages, foreign education is not so widespread as to influence the existing beliefs. And because in these remote areas, whatever education is available has favored boys over girls, it is likely that males would be the ones exposed to some level of elementary yovo education, but not high enough to free them from the possibility of syncretism or double belonging. In villages, it is likely that most but especially the less formally educated girls will have one foot in one religious world and another foot in the other.

A focus on the role of "compatible parts" is one helpful addition to the idea of ethnogenesis. Inculturation, which means new yovo culture infused in the native original and "made fresh through its incorporation into the worldviews and liturgical practices of indigenous cultures," is not double belonging. And

double religious belonging is not ethnogenesis, earlier defined as one of the outcomes of inculturation.

> At best, hybrid religion has been seen in terms of the language of 'syncretism,'
> where aggregations of unlikes are held together more by circumstance than by
> their own cultural logic and thus prove unstable and of only fleeting conse-
> quence. . . .'[I]nculturation,' [is] where the Christian faith is made fresh
> through its incorporation into the worldviews and liturgical practices of indige-
> nous cultures (McNally, 2000: 844).

Double belonging and syncretism are not ethnogenesis, but they may signal the
beginning of the rise of ethnicity. In other words, it may be possible to concep-
tualize ethnogenesis as a continuum that begins with the original religion, progressively moves to syncretism and double belonging, and eventually to the
birth of a new fluid identity due to more and more inculturation. The ethnogenesis framework helps explain well but also predict the religious hybridity evident
in the reports of many interviewees. But inculturation is still in its infancy, and
so is the process of ethnogenesis. Moreover, not all Beninese scholars agree with
the value of inculturation.

Beninese scholars on inculturation.

There has been a debate about this issue between two self-identified Christians—Roger Gbegnonvi and Barthélemy Adoukounou (see Publications du
Sillon Noir). Gbegnonvi hopes for the disappearance of traditional religion and
highlights the necessity for Beninese men and women to look for "nouveaux
repères" [new benchmarks] as not to "soon disappear in the rumbles of history"
(1998: 1). The Fon of the South are controlled by Vodun and what he calls *la
bouffe*, reason why they refuse the call and pathway that leads to Mawu.
    According to this train of thought, ethnogenesis is not only influenced by
education and generation but also everyday life and above all by food, a basic
necessity. As Gbegnonvi argues, a question raised often by the Fon is: "Y-a-t-il
a manger là-dedans?" (Is there food in this?). Everything involved involves
food. If one sells something that one owns, "ce n'est pas pour investir ailleurs
que dans la bouffe." [it is not to invest anywhere else but in *la bouffe*] (see
Adoukonou, 1998: 2). Finally, Gbegnonvi (Adoukonou, 1998: 3) goes as far as
to say

> si pour l'Occidental l'homme est un animal pensant, pour le Fon, il est 'un
> animal mangeur de sel.' Les Fon convertis au catholicisme romain n'ont retenu
> du baptême que le rite de manducation du sel, qui est pourtant loin d'être
> constitutif du sacrement concerné. . . . Pour le Fon, être baptisé se dit 'duje'
> (manger le sel), et le baptême se dit 'jedudu' (manducation du sel).
> [if for the Occidental man is a thinking animal, for the Fon, man is "an animal
> eater of salt." The Fon who converts to Roman Catholicism have only retained
> from baptism the rite of manducation of salt, though it is far from being consti-

tutive of this sacrament. . . For the Fon, to be baptized is expressed with 'duje' (eating salt) and the baptism is said 'jedudu' (manducation of salt)]

Harsh or not, biased or not, the argument sends an important message about popular Catholicism in Benin, that an inculturated religion will retain from a culture what it considers essential—including, in this case, its food aspect. If the statement is correct it also supports points made earlier about elements compatible versus the incompatible in inculturation. Baptismal rites have retained the salt considered important and compatible with basic societal values.

Developing further his argument about values, Gbegnonvi suggests what is important to the Fon is not life itself as one cannot eat life. And he blames the system Vodun for encouraging this attitude toward *la bouffe*.

le vodun est à l'origine d'un système ou l'égoïsme est cultivé et pratiqué jusqu'à sa dernière conséquence impliquant la mort de l'autre pour le triomphe de soi. . . . Un tel system transforme nécessairement la société en un champ clos de suspicion généralisé et conduit . . . à la banalisation du crime (Adoukonou 1998: 6).

[Vodun is at origin of a system where egoism is nurtured and practiced, until its final consequence which implicates death of the other for the triumph of self. Such a system necessarily transforms the society into an enclosed field of generalized suspicion and leads. . . to the vulgarisation of crime]

With this quote, we are reminded of the priest convert who in a previous chapter, explained the difference between religion Vodun and what he referred to as system Vodou.

To change focus from *la bouffe*, the Fon must turn to Mawu who has the attributes of God but also those generally attributed to women, including tenderness. The problem, he writes, is there is no temple specifically to honor Mawu. This absent place of worship is because of the Fon's refusal of Mawu and her ideals. Inculturation derails from progress. For this scholar, assimilation into Catholicism would be the superior outcome. A religious ethnogenesis that does not lead to the cult of Mawu or the disappearance of such values as *la bouffe* would not be his preference. Gbénonvi is highly critical of inculturation.

There is a counter argument presented by Abbé Barthélemy Adoukonou. Adoukonou is a strong avocate of inculturation who argues, "La tâche de reconstruction de l'Afrique demande que les Africains se réconcilient avec leur propre histoire et avec leur propre culture." [The task of reconstructing Africa requires that Africans reconcile with their own history and with their own culture] Accusing Gbénonvi of following European thinkers, refusing "l'héritage noir," and self-hatred, Adoukonou relates inculturation to incarnation. "La création n'a pas été totalement corrompue par le péché, elle a conservé un fond bon qui s'exprime dans les cultures.» [Creation has not been completely spoiled by sin, it has kept a good foundation that is expressed in cultures] (Adoukonou 1998: 12).

Adoukonou also suggest that Gbénonvi is de-sacralising the sacred ancestors, and proposes an alternative frame for the analysis—that of Claude Lévi-Strauss. Focusing primarily on the issue of "la bouffe," Adoukonou argues, the sons of Africa labor to survive despite limited material resources. Their survival is due to "ethical resources" of endurance. These traditional ethnic resources must be appropriated.

Adoukonou (1998: 16)explains the purpose of *Sillon Noir* [Black Furrow] (*Méwihwendo*): to see a "Chrétien Africain."

Il s'agit pour l'Homme Noir de reprendre l'initiative historique avec vigueur et rigueur en partant du potentiel culturel . . . Les deux, l'Intéllectuel Universitaire et l'Intéllectuel Communautaire, sont appelés à promouvoir l'interculturalité, l'interrationalité, l'interhistoricité, bref à apprendre et à initier à la «culture du lien».

[It is a question of the Black Man recapturing the historical initiative with vigor and rigor starting from the cultural potential. . . . Both, the university intellectual and the public intellectual are called to promote interculturality, interrationality, interhistoricity, in sum to learn and to initiate the "culture of link"].

According to Adoukonou, *Méwihwendo* would lead to an Africanization of Christianity and would produce "un Chrétien Africain."

As demonstrated here, scholars differ on the benefits of inculturation. The debate between Adoukonou and Gbénonvi representing the two sides suggests a disagreement as to the acceptable levels and direction of ethnogenesis. We would expect the views of other scholars to fall between these two extremes.

Most educated Beninese received a Catholic education. Inculturation would promote the rise of a new ethnicity by transforming these Christians into African Christians. Theirs would be a popular Catholicism that includes compatible elements of traditional culture and religion. But also as predicted by ethnogenesis, some Beninese would practice a close to pure Catholicism while most fall along a continuum of inculturated religion. The more intense parochial education is, the less likely they would be to include the incompatible in their practice.

But as Adepoju has shown, generation will have a major influence on the direction of ethnogenesis. New elements which fit the existing culture will have a much better chance of growth and survival when successfully sifted through the family system. Educational and generational influences will continue to compete for space on the religious ethnogenesis of the Beninese, unless of course the wishes of the Vodun dignitary become reality and traditional education is widespread. In this case, the generational segment will be even stronger as it modifies the direction of religious and cultural development. The words of Bolaji Idowu (1973: 203) are again appropriate in this finale.

One of two things has happened to man's religion in any given situation: modification with adaptation, or extinction. The first may be said to have been the fate of religion throughout the world, of any religion. There is no religion that has not taken into itself elements from other religio-cultures. Influences from other cultures and contacts with immigrant religions have brought, not only changes in the complexion of religion, but also modification of its tenets. The most particular religions have not been able to escape this factor: they have been forced by the nature of things to give and take elements to and from even those religious which they regard as their enemies or rivals.

This, I found the nature of the Catholic imagination in Benin.

Conclusion

This chapter considered the outcome of religious interaction and the impact of general forces (including extended family power) on negotiating religious borders from double-belonging to inculturation. Not all Beninese scholars agree on the value of inculturation but regardless of their position on the issue, inculturation seems inavoidable. The questions may be only, how much and how fast is inculturation.

Though it appears that education also plays a role in negotiating religious borders, the impact of generational forces on religious retention and change cannot be overestimated. Catholicism in Benin has multiple faces, each a variation and the result of family power.

Chapter Five
What We Learned

To gain insights into Beninese Catholicism and its influence on social justice was one of the goals of this study. If religion—any religion—appears influencing openness to the other and openness promotes social justice, then it is useful to dig up elements likely to occasion the openness and justice. Studying different expressions of a religious practice brings to the fore its consistent features, its ideal type, its key elements having the openness consequence. To this task, Catholicism is especially useful because universal. One comment heard most often from self-identified Catholics interviewed in the Midwest in early and mid-2000 was, whenever traveling outside the United States no matter how foreign that culture, that they could count on the familiarity and soothing comfort of their catholic practice. In unfamiliar surroundings, Catholicism was their familiar. Even when these Americans disagreed with aspects of the practice (many fit that category), or if they were not fluent in the language of a visited country, they could follow the rituals of Mass given essentials of which they say, openness to the other is a part.

Using everyday life in Benin as a case study, I sought to explain what it means to be Catholic, and implications that identity holds for the acceptance of otherness. But ideas guiding this work are much broader. They go beyond a single religion. Catholicism is important to the extent it is global and concerned with social justice. In the United States where Sunday services tend to be segregated, researchers find Catholic churches cross-racial and communitarian. I decided to see if openness to others also held outside the United States, specifically West Africa—an often neglected corner of the world where Christianity is vibrant and where vocations are growing rapidly especially in comparison with western countries such as France or the United States.

Interviews from selected Beninese cities of the South acknowledge the tendency among Catholics to mix religious practices. As one respondent said "even Muslims do it." Most informants (including Catholics) think Catholics visit temples of traditional religion and speak of friends who reveal they do.

These informants are aware also of their own parents making such visits. But most go beyond these reflections as they offer reasons other than syncretism for the apparent mix. They mention the lack of conviction, intellectual curiosity, studying another faith, and a plea for immediate spiritual relief not answered by the Catholic Church due to priests who see the faithful solely by appointment.

Lack of conviction is mentioned most often as primary reason for mixing practices. Catholic respondents note, members of groupings such as the *Renouveau Charismatique Catholique* [Catholic Charismatic Renewal] do not double-belong pointing thus to the importance of involvement in one's dedication to a particular faith, and choice between syncretism and inculturation.[30] The more intense involvement, the more committed to religious groupings, the less the need for an alternative religious world. Such groupings provide a more intense experience of God (see Wutnow, 1994).

But where religious groupings strengthen faith, kin may still influence practice. As with the couple not successful in bearing a child, the authority of kinship may induce utter confusion. In a society where family matters and "children are one of the primary means of attaining status for women" (Madhavan, 2001: 512), extended kin pushed this couple to seek help outside the Catholic faith, confronting them with a heavy burden, a dilemma, and leading them to seek guidance from their priest. If accepting the recommendation of family the couple proceeded to consult a traditional healer or engaged in rituals not sanctioned by their faith, they would have walked through the door of the other. But this move originating from external sources (family) having been forced, would not appropriately reflect the influence either direct or indirect of Catholic teachings on diversity. In fact, such actions would cross the very boundaries set by the couple's faith.

It is obvious to the Beninese that Catholics are mixing religious practices as everyone else. But asked about their own practice, what do Catholics themselves say? Do they mix? Their answers to the question are clear and firm: no, they do not. Indeed for support, we could return to the couple for whom the very thought of mixing translated into a personal dilemma, a clash between personal and family values. Catholic respondents say sometimes they visit other churches only because invited for a wedding, funeral or other such occasions. As for temples of the traditional religion, they never visit.

Acknowledgement of occasional visits to other churches suggests some openness to the other even partial only, given the exclusion of traditional temples. But the acknowledgements also fall far from the general perception of a Catholic trend to syncretize—a trend attested to by Catholics and traditionalists alike when speaking of the general population. Following are examples of response by traditionalists on this issue:

> Il y a beaucoup de gens qui se disaient catholique mais au fond ils pratiquaient le Vodun. Pour vous convaincre . . . bon . . . dans la journée ils sont des Catholiques mais dans la soirée nous les verrons. . . . Il faut voir les catholiques qui viennent me voir la nuit!

[There are many people who were saying they are Catholic but deep down they were practicing Vodun. . . . To convince, well, during the day they are Catholic but in the evening we will see them. . . . You have to see the Catholics who come to see me at night.]

When I asked these devotees of traditional religion if I could see a record of Catholics they insist visit in the dark of the night, I was told there is no documentation—not surprising in this oral culture where *la parole* [the word] is sacred. Such record provided would raise suspicion indeed, given the prevailing orality.

Moreover, if record keeping were normative and documentation of visits available, for obvious reasons Catholics might not visit or insist their visits not be recorded. My own observation is like Haitians, the Beninese tend to have discretion about daily activities. I was often told in Benin that if four people know something about someone, everyone in the country already knows it. The thought that written records could possibly find their way into wrong hands would cap what visitors reveal. Potential visitors might refrain altogether from seeking help in the tradition. So, *la parole* suffices. *La parole* is sacred, honored, and sealed—just a drop of water on the ground. Without written record, the visits and their object are known only to visitors, those whom they visit and, of course, their ancestors.

As seen earlier, the family exerts pressures on members or at least strongly encourages help-seeking outside the Catholic faith. Hence it is likely even those who belong to religious groupings said to enhance commitment to a single faith will undergo, at times yield to, these pressures and encouragements. But chances are committed Catholics will inculturate more so than syncretize, or might observe some traditions during important family gatherings as a show of respect for their elders. The medical professional who after placing money in the sacred hole, head bowed and eyes closed followed the prayers of her aunt, did so out of respect even as she, staunch Catholic, recited the Divine Office before attending daily Mass.

A former Catholic, now devotee of traditional religion, explains this controlling role of the family in what happens before a funeral takes place:

Si quelqu'un meurt, c'est le catholique qui meurt, le prêtre arrive et il fait leurs prières. Bon, il enterre la personne. Après avoir enterré la personne, on pratique notre religion—la tradition des ancients. Bon maintenant, pour convaincre, si quelqu'un meurt, il est catholique il meurt maintenant, bon, il pratique la religion catholique seul et après, au fond dans leur famille, ils vous font ce qu'il faut faire.

[If someone dies, well it is a Catholic who dies, the priest arrives and he says prayers. After burying the person, they practice our religion—the ancient tradition. Now to convince, if someone dies, he is catholic and now he dies, well he practices the catholic religion alone and after that, within their family, they make you do what is to be done].

Here again, the family's authority and imposition of tradition is evidenced even in death. One illustration is the case of a catholic religious professional whose close relative had recently died. During planning stages of the funeral, he had enormous difficulty convincing family members in attendance that this relative for whom he cared during the last weeks of life did not, would not, want a traditional ceremony, that the funeral and burial should be strictly Catholic—nothing more, nothing less. Though he succeeded eventually, his quest difficult at best left him clearly disturbed, exhausted and saddened by the family's first reactions and his having to advocate so forcefully for the dead.

Occasionally Catholics return to the tradition without pressure from family and strictly for personal reasons. Such a return may be in desperate situations as in the case of a terminal illness, a curable disease for which modern medicine has not reached the African land, in case of infertility in a society where having children is so valued childless households are perceived deviant, or, again, if the person affected by disease (and his/her entourage) believes he/she to be the target of *envoûtement* (sorcery). In such situations, those who revisit are likely seeking limited, specific and immediate relief outside Catholic practices wherever can be located. Especially if holding membership in religious groupings, this search for limited help is without embracing or "brassing" other parts of the tradition.

These reasons for occasional Catholic returns to the tradition would also bridge the gap between statements of respondents about Catholic mixing that seem at odds with the statements of Catholics about their own practice. But again, the coming-and-going seems influenced more by a tight hold of the extended family on members, and beliefs in the necessity to acquire through traditional worship the blessings of ancestors. Who in the society would want to lose these blessings? Eventually, however, a process of inculturation is likely to take place where compatible elements become standard practice of popular Catholicism—part of the process of ethnogenesis and, in this case, a sort of beninesation of Catholicism.

Previous comments show strained moments in the coexistence of traditional religion with Christianity. Worth reemphasizing is how through kin, traditional forces represented by family pull in the Catholic (and other) faithful. But beyond the forces of tradition, pulling in may be eased also by knowledge of past (perhaps also present) physical and financial help provided by adepts of the tradition for the construction of churches, as in the *Immaculée Conception* Cathedral of Ouidah. While Catholicism would like to push out the traditional practices (though not as forcefully as Protestant sects, especially Evangelicals based upon interviews with Evangelicals, and with Vodun adepts), Vodun religion seems to pull in Catholicism.[31] We heard from a Daah, hurt by his own biological brother-priest's absence from traditional ceremonies even as this Daah, himself, welcomes attending Christian churches. He asks his biological brother and other Christians (especially devotees of Protestant sects): "Why do you refuse to eat with me even as I eat with you?" To him, eating together would demonstrate trust and acceptance of his religion. Yet, for Catholics, eating during traditional religious ceremonies would symbolize syncretism and double belonging. As in other areas of everyday life, the very same act takes on different meanings from different standpoints. Sometimes at least in the open, Catholics seem to favor the *either or* dichotomy typical of western thought (Brown, 1989) while Protestants appear more consistent dichotomists. Devotees of traditional religion favor fluidity in their religious practice thus avoiding or lessening tensions provoked by the dichotomy.

The inculturation (not syncretism) of Catholic practices seems one resolution. By the way reverse inculturation is also occurring at the level of Vodun. By reverse inculturation I mean the insertion of Catholic symbols and language in traditional ceremonies. Vodun devotees use terms from Catholic vocabulary to refer to their services. Sometimes, they will speak of Sunday Mass, confession, communion, benediction, priest, church, blessed water, baptism, convent. I was told by one informant, sometimes during services it is difficult to know what type of church one is attending, if it is a Catholic Mass or a traditional religious ceremony. At least one Daah-respondent was proud of the fact that his children attended a Catholic school.

Once I was invited to a traditional (Vodou) Church service in the city Cotonou. From the loft where I sat, with bare feet as expected, I was able to see indeed many Catholic rites integrated in the service. Here, I might also mention several Daahs during their interviews who expressed love for the late Pope John Paul II, stressed the Pope's show of respect for them when he removed his shoes, posed for pictures, and spent time with them during his visit to Benin in the early 90s. The Pope's presence among them was a clear indication of openness to the other, as well as an invitation to follow this example. Pope John Paul II seemed more open to the adherents of traditional religion, than are Catholics in their own practice, or willing to admit about that practice. For his interview, one Daah sat proudly next to a framed portrait of Pope John Paul II joined by adherents of traditional religion.

While Catholics seem to accept the religious other based upon occasional visits to non-Catholic churches and, as reported by some adepts of traditional religion, Catholics' occasional consultations with a Daah, most devotees of traditional religion seem more open to other faiths, especially Catholicism, at a more intense level of interaction. It is doubtful that Catholics in Benin especially from religious groupings would go so far as help build a Vodun temple, display a picture of the Supreme Chief in their homes or, if they existed, send their children to Vodun schools. Catholics would not approve of their children's marriage to an adept of traditional religion.

Marriage: Inter-ethnic, Inter-religious and International

Attitudes toward inter-ethnic, inter-religious, and international marriage of one's children can also inform about openness to the other. These attitudes shed light on the come-and-go religious practice, according to a majority of respondents is the case in Benin.

The interviews show all faiths receptive to the possibility of an inter-ethnic marriage for their loved ones. Often, to show proof of acceptance, the respondents speak of their own unions to someone from a different ethnic group or the interethnic marriage of their children. This marriage appears not to pose a problem. But the outcome may have been different if the question, which was general, targeted specific ethnic groups.

Inter-religious marriage is more complex. Most adepts of traditional religion are open to their children's marriage to other adepts, to Catholics, and to Muslims. They seem less open to a marriage with Evangelicals and would prefer it if their children did not marry members of the Celestial Church.

Few Catholics are open to marriage with traditionalists or members of the Celestial Church of Christ, but prefer marriage to other Catholics. It is interesting, too, having said 'yes' to the idea of intermarriage, if asked how they would feel if their daughter or son married someone from traditional religion, their response tends to begin with two words . . .*Ca la* . . . [. . . That . . .] taking time to think before presenting their attitudes. There is also a vocal stress on *Ca la*. They hesitate before and after *Ca la*, taking the additional time to formulate an answer. Clearly, Catholics do not accept this marriage as they do the other types. But, Catholic or not, almost all respondents emphasize happiness and well-being. Though they would prefer a Catholic son- or daughter-in-law and may not fully agree to a daughter or son's marriage to Evangelicals or Muslims (but especially Evangelicals judged too strict and close-minded in their attitudes toward them and other non Evangelicals,) eventually these Catholics would accept whatever is their children's choice of mate including from traditional religion.

Muslims would accept marriage with a Catholic but only in case of later conversion to Islam even as many interviewed, including an Imam, expressed closeness to Catholics and Catholicism. Evangelicals who say they take the words of the Bible literally were least open to their children's marriage to a different faith, including Catholics many critiqued for "worshiping statues and images like Vodun adepts." This form of worship, the Evangelicals thought of as idolatry. They did not appear to accept the ideas of symbolic representation, of images, statues and other evidence of sacramental imagination.[32] But, as most other respondents, they too are concerned with the well-being of their children and would accept what makes them happy.

As for international marriage, most respondents say yes and would accept their children's choice of an American African or American European, though in case of a white, one adept of traditional religion would insist on the couple living closer geographically to the African side of family. Several respondents asked about the religious affiliation of this European or African American, an affiliation in their view might make a difference in how they view such a marriage. This reservation was not expected since informants mention in Benin, marrying white an honor sought after. By the way, most respondents would prefer an American to a French perhaps because, in general, the Beninese interviewed do not think positively of *la France*. It is a nation many consider racist and concerned with its own interests rather than the good of Africans. On several occasions, I heard the Beninese express a wish to have been colonized by the English. Providing the example of Anglophone territories such as Ghana, they suggest under such protectorate, their country would be more developed economically.

Almost all respondents have a special love for the United States they think is a blessed country. In particular, they mention entrepreneurship and the generosity of Americans. While a few, especially better educated, raised the issue of American racism reported to them by the Beninese who visit, most respondent say they feel close to the United States because it has within it an extension of West Africa. There is an "Africa" in the United States. Those who never visited look forward some day to that experience. But preference for an American marriage expressed, the respondents would accept whatever marriage makes their children happy.

If inter-religious and international marriages are barometers of openness to the other, the adepts of Vodun religion are most open and least open are Evangelicals. Catholics come close to traditionalists. As for international marriage, the adepts of Vodun religion for whom re-valorizing the tradition is pivotal are least open to it but also insist eventually on accepting whatever choice is their children's. Indeed this comment was a theme repeated countless times, even after the respondents had objected to some types of unions due to geographical or cultural distancing from kin.

Perhaps an indicator of openness other than interethnic, inter-religious and international marriage, one more sensitive to the Beninese culture might produce different results. The Evangelicals I met were diligent when it came to helping me gather people for an interview or handing out questionnaires, even as they knew my association with Catholicism and the goals of my research. In the second chapter, I mentioned how the wife of an Evangelical Pastor, a Pastor who later would be instrumental in coordinating interviews, agreed to come with me to help locate the residence that she shared with her husband. This wife and I met by happenstance in a store, as I stopped there to ask for directions to the Pastor's house. As previously indicated, the Pastor himself was very helpful. After the interviews I conducted at his residence, he offered further unsolicited help with contacts, if I needed to speak with more Evangelicals anywhere in, or even outside of Benin.

It is similar for members of the Celestial Church who coordinated interviews for me with several members of their Church although in Cotonou a few chose not return the questionnaires distributed. (There was a similar episode in another city for reasons having to do with financial remuneration. In the case of Celestial Church members, the reasons appeared different though not openly stated). In general, regardless of religious affiliation, all groups were pleased with this research on the sacramental imagination and willing to help in whatever way they could to make it succeed.

Catholicism and Social Justice

The connection between Catholicism and social justice another goal of this work is blurred and requires additional research. The Catholic Church is very active in Benin with hospitals, clinics, schools, orphanages, and such agencies as *Caritas* (Catholic Charities) serving the general population regardless of religious affiliation. Moreover, whether traditionalists, Evangelicals, Catholics, Muslims, or members of the Celestial Church of Christ, the respondents almost unanimously offer high praise for the Catholic Church when acknowledging this generous service to everyone. When asked to evaluate Catholic social service to the community, most respondents say it is very important. However, I found a direct link between popular Catholicism and social justice difficult to establish due to the coexistence of faiths each claiming *l'amour de l'autre* [love of the other] and social justice as part of their teachings and practice. If the availability of social services to all regardless of religious affiliation or ability to pay were taken as a sole or primary indicator of openness to the other, Catholics would be highest on a scale of social justice. Future research will need to refine the indicators of social justice and select those that are better suited to a West African settings.

Diaspora: African Americans/Haitian Americans

Still another goal of this study was to assign meaning to the everyday habits of two diaspora populations—African Americans and Haitian Americans. I found this goal much more complex and as with the link between popular Catholicism and social justice, requiring additional time and research. This study can only offer ideas to be investigated further about what might account for differences between African Americans and Haitian Americans.

Some historical facts are clear and uncontested: African men, women and children were brought in chains, thus by force to the Western Hemisphere for unpaid work on plantations. Tears roll out of my eyes when I travelled along what is now known as the *Slave Route* going from *Place Cha-Cha* to *La Porte du Non-Retour,* near the ocean where long ago boats with Christian names awaited real human beings for the transatlantic voyage. Other visitors communicate a similar experience. Today despite being modernized the historical road cannot be journeyed by foot because too long and rough. Visitors go by means of transportation. Yet heavily chained men, women, and children in inhumane physical and psychological circumstances were obliged to do so. Even the most imaginative of minds would have difficulty reconstructing the barbarous events, what went through the minds and lashed bodies of these humans as they moved away from motherland and family to unknown destinations. That so many survived the savagery is a conundrum. They took with them only the non-material—memories of family, of place, of culture, of religion. African diaspora populations in the United States, Haiti, Brazil, Cuba, and elsewhere share these ancestral experiences and links with each other and the people of West Africa.

On the island of Hispaniola centuries ago, the enslaved battled vigorously and successfully for liberation. They fought French troops not with arms but with religion and culture. They were also helped by their numerical majority over whites. From the rubble of this revolution and from memories of kin, religion, cuisine, these freedmen carved a new way of life as closely as possible to the African, yet a life lacking from the old because in the midst of new realities such as separation from family—the backbone of any society. Family was especially important here because rooted in ancestral culture. The freedmen tried filling the environmental and cultural gaps with whatever was immediately obtainable. They adapted old milieu to new surroundings. They assigned their own meanings to the new.[33] According to legend, the famous Haitian *soup joumou* (also called yellow soup, or *soupe giraumon*) helped celebrate the sweeping victory. Today for many Haitians and Haitian immigrants around the world, this ritual still marks the turn from an enslaved past. During captivity, French masters savored the tempting *soupe giraumon* while the enslaved guzzled more basic foods. This restriction changed after the revolution when given new meaning. *Soupe giraumon* became *soup joumou*. Symbol of freedom and equality, it is eaten at least on the first day of January. *Soup joumou* (sometimes referred to as *soupe jaune* or *Independence Day soup*) along with the national blue and red flag (the red, white and blue flag of France with the white removed) became indicators of Haitians beating the odds, "colonizing the French," and turning things around (see Bob Corbett).[34]

The outcome of the Haitian Revolution was an example of success so powerful, the rest of the free world thought it necessary to isolate these newly freedmen from other enslaved, such as in the United States. How could black slaves have dared such actions? How could they win a battle against heavily armed French soldiers? How could they have defeated Napoleon? Feeling threatened, the free world could not afford an imitation of this horrifying event. And to teach a lesson to others who would ever try, France taxed the formerly enslaved for their daring actions. Haiti was forced to indemnify France for her loss. This too signaled France right to the ownership of human beings complete with their labor power and labor, thus her right to chattel slavery. I believe some day once her conscience has fully matured, that France will reimburse to the people of Haiti, at least, in part this historical robbery. But reparation besides, the successful revolution turned enslaved Africans into Haitians. France's St. Domingue was now Haitians' *Hayti*.[35] Today's Haitians with ancestry in Africa are not Africans. Haitianization begins with the Independence of 1804 of which Haitians continue to be proud. With this historical marker begins the shaping of new identities and a new chapter in the history of this first black nation's collective memory (see Bob Corbett).[36]

But despite the implantation and progressive growth of the new national character, there remained and still remain many similarities between West Africa and Haiti. In the first part of this work, I cite authors who unveiled many points of resemblance between the two peoples. More recent writings also acknowledge

> [t]he majority of Haiti's enslaved Africans had been deported from there [Benin]. Numerous scholars have observed that this Dahomean cultural continuity is very obvious in Haiti. . . . For instance the anthropologist Alfred Métraux identified similarities in their religious practices and economic structures. He also noticed striking resemblance in physical appearance, in gestures, and behavior patterns between Haitians and Dahomeans (Fandrich 2005: 38-39).

I also explain in my own personal experience many noticeable connections. Longtime geographical, cultural and political isolation from the developed world have positively impacted Haitian retention of West African culture. Today while globalization has somewhat lessened the separation, Haiti is still isolated because marginalized (see Bellegarde-Smith, 2007). Culturally, Haitians blend well in Benin, a blend further helped by French colonization of both countries. Benin's independence from France came in August 1960. In Benin, a large Haitian community reports feeling at home. This is especially the case for those directly from Haiti who may be mistaken for Beninese. The noted Dr. Conceptia Ouinsou, former Supreme Court Justice in Benin recently intronized Princess of the Royal Court of Allada was born, raised and received her education in Haiti before earning the doctorate in France. Her position as Supreme Court Justice came despite her birth outside of Benin. When Dr. Ouinsou appears on television wearing her tall elegant *atchoke* and African attire or when communicating with the public it is difficult to know her Haitian origins. She is Beninese indeed; but also Haitian. She functions comfortably in more than one world and represents the common family name shared by Haiti and Benin. Dr. Ouinsou is not *either* Haitian *or* Beninese, but *both* Haitian and Beninese.

Haitians in Benin are especially attached to the city of Allada where stands a giant statue of Toussaint l'Ouverture with the inscription "Général Toussaint L'Ouverture, digne fils d'Allada." [General Toussaint L'Ouverture, worthy son of Allada]. Gaou Guinou, Toussaint's great grandfather was captured, enslaved by the French and taken to the plantation Breda on the Island of Hispaniola where Toussaint was born. On the wall of Allada's King Kpodégbé Toyi Djigla's palace are a wood carving of the Haitian flag with its motto *L'union fait la force*. Also displayed on the wall are several pictures of Haitians made dignitaries of the Royal Court of Allada and a group photo of Haitian President René Préval and Mrs. Préval, with the King and Queen Djéhami his wife who serves as Minister of Culture. Once a year, official celebrations take place in the square where stands Toussaint's sculpture. The celebrations, below flying Haitian and

Beninese flags, include sacred dances and tam-tams, with vivid colors, chanting and other sacred sounds that imprint the mind deeply long after these ceremonies have concluded. In attendance are kings and queens, diplomats and, most importantly, the people. The purpose of these ceremonies is to renew and strengthen cultural identity. During the course of one such ceremony which I attended, I heard Toussaint referred to as Beninese-Haitian. While some may disagree with this identity assigned to the General who was born on St Domingue's Plantation Bréda—not in Dahomey, there is no denying the connection between the two populations. Here are similarities shared with Dr. Ouinsou.

I was fortunate enough to have two audiences with King Kpodégbé at the Royal Palace in Allada. The King considers Allada the birth home of Haitians and invites them to the land of their roots. During my meetings with him at the Palace, he consistently referred to me as "Princesse Yanick." I felt honored. But in my own mind, this form of address coming from the King was one way for him to disrupt even momentarily the historical and geographical gaps that separate Haitians from their origins in Allada and the rest of West Africa. It was one way to bridge the centuries-gap that separates a descendant of the enslaved from her ancestors.

To those who refer to Toussaint as Beninese-Haitian, birth outside of West Africa is irrelevant to African identity. It is similar to the birth of Conceptia Ouinsou in Haiti. Slave captivity may have disrupted the material links between origin and destination but in force is a memory. Today erected next to the ocean in the city of Ouidah, the *door-of-no-return* is turned around. It has become its reverse or the *door-of-return*. The African diaspora visit and revisit. And they like the experience. There is continuity. The bonds remain. Alive is a collective memory of place and extended family. Toussaint's identity is transnational. This recognition of transnationality may already be put in practice for the larger Haitian population. While I was still in Benin, changes in immigration law were in progress whereby Haitians would no longer need a visa to enter that country. Haitians who come to Benin and to Allada specifically have come to their extended home.

Thus the conquest of slavery and the rise of an independent island nation of West Africans abroad have not suppressed parentage. By the way, on many occasions the people in Benin apologized to me for their contributions to slavery—something I never heard in the United States or anywhere else. Introspective and regardless of class aware of that past, the Beninese are open about their elite's participation in the trade but make responsibility their own. Deeply regretting the past, they make no excuse and recognize it is their ancestors, too, who left the African land. Sometimes when shopping at the open market, I would share with women vendors my Haitian origins. Immediately they would express regret about the trade in comments equivalent to: We have not treated you well. We are glad you have returned to your home. Welcome back, *Bienvenue*, they would add. At that point, I was no longer considered a *yovo* (foreigner) but one of them, their alter ego, although they would tell me jokingly that I am an *aguda* (not pure type). Having been identified as one of them, the prices of fruits and vegetables would also go down, closer, I assume, to prices set for local people than for *yovos* (especially white). There is a price for the Beninese, another for the *yovo*.

For some researchers, similarities between Haiti and Benin are most obvious in the practice of traditional religion and popular Catholicism. Traditional religion made its voyage to the island of Hispaniola. Alfred Métraux writes while some Haitians practice "pure" Catholicism, in Haiti "Catholicisme et Vodou n'ont pas de frontières interdites. 'Il faut être catholique pour server les loas.'" [Catholicism and Vodun have no forbidden frontiers. One must be Catholic to serve the gods].[37] This suggests in Haiti, the practice of a syncretized Catholicism, more obvious in the masses who do not hide hybridity, with a version more fluid for the educated upper and middle classes (see also Herskovits, 1937).

Despite Métraux's overgeneralization, his ideas support points earlier in this work that the lower the level of education, the lesser impact of imported religion; the more intense education the more likely the inculturation of compatible practices. Recall the basis tenets of ethnogenesis—the influences of education and generation give birth to ethnicity. Various levels of inculturation at various levels of education and passing of generations would also be expected. Of course occasionally, increasing inculturation would not eliminate features perceived incompatible at first, as for example consultations with a *bokonon* (traditional medicine man) when disease strikes the family, or in case of infertility when intense prayer and other Christian rituals do not appear to bring the swift relief that is sought. At such critical moments one uses whatever is at one's fingertips—tradition or modernity—whatever practice works, including the previously-thought incompatible—just in case. Turning to the incompatible is especially likely when family pressures are at work.

Family disruptions.

One important difference between the Haitian and Beninese situations may be in the weight of extended family's influence over retention or rejection of religious practices. The Beninese extended family, an expansion of generations, has what Adepoju describes as "two visions of the world." The double vision is the outcome of colonization. Double vision is at the intersection of "imported" and traditional religions. In the following statement, a Daah who often speaks of such issues on the Catholic radio of Benin (*Radio Immaculée* in Allada) and wants to be identified, proposes the meeting of these two visions bears the separation of kin—a reality causing him frustrations.

> Comment on peut expliquer vous êtes venu chez moi . . . demain vous pouvez arriver, nous avons noué une relation, je suis tout le temps chez vous et je vous demande d'aller vers moi et vous refusez. D'abord vous rentrez chez quelqu'un, vous lui dites: 'changez votre nom, votre nom c'est diabolique. Ne mangez plus cela, ça la, c'est diabolique. Ne faites plus cette pratique de votre

culture, ça la, c'est mauvais. 'La sortie des enfants,' ne faites plus. Votre maison, il y a trop de sorciers,' et vous opposez l'enfant à son papa, l'enfant à sa mère. Or c'est bien le papa qui a accepté que son enfant soit baptisé. Et le premier jour en même temps après le baptême on lui dit de ne plus mettre pied dans sa maison.

[[How is it possible to explain that you came to my house . . . tomorrow you can come, we have developed a relation, I am always in your house and I asked you to come to me, and you refuse. First of all, you come into someone house, you tell them: 'change your name, your name is diabolical; don't ever eat that, that is diabolical; don't practice this aspect of your culture, that is bad. The presentation of children, do not do it anymore. In your house, there are too many sorcerers' and you oppose a child to his father, a child to his mother; yet it is the father who has accepted that his child be baptized]

Daah provides specific examples of what triggers his disappointment and pain. Family is critical in the Beninese context. As he sees it, family separations are nurtured by Catholicism, but even more so the multitudes of Protestant sects currently planted and blooming in Benin due to commercialism. As he sees it, ethnocentric (mostly Protestant) sects diabolize the traditional faith and culture. He is Daah—a priest in the Vodun religion, but his own biological brother is Father—a Catholic priest. As he sees it, this traditional/modern religious split common in Africa, appearing to the outsider as a religious democracy, is tension-producing.

[On dit que le Bénin est laïc, mais la réalité] c'est quelque chose qui a été imposé . . . et nous avons accepté, c'est tout. C'est pas qu'au départ nous sommes un pays laïc, non. Combien de religions il y a [au Bénin]? Il y a seulement Vodun. C'est après que les autres religions sont arrivées, même les musulmans, c'est après qu'ils sont arrivés. Donc, on n'est pas du tout un pays laïc. Mais comme la colonisation est arrivée on nous a imposé ça, nous avons accepté nous avons accepté maintenant et on nous refuse maintenant de pratiquer notre religion.

[People say that Benin is a democracy but reality is it is something that have been imposed and we have accepted. that's all. It is not that at first we are a lay country, no. It is not that at first we are a lay country, no. How many religions are there? There is only Vodun. It is after that other religions have come. Even Muslims, it is after that they arrived. So we are not a laic country. But since colonization has arrived and imposed that, we have accepted and now they refuse for us to practice our religion.

Stressing further the regrettable outcome of a double vision and domination of one over the other, Daah also provides the example of a woman in a state of trance whose pearls and other religious articles are taken from her by order of a priest—though he fails to indicate if this priest is Beninese or foreign extraction.

mais quelqu'un est en train de faire sa religion la femme qui est en transe le
prêtre qui est là-bas il est parti envoyer des gens. On l'a ramené et il a détruit
les perles, les instruments de vaudous que la femme a. Ca veut dire nous ne
sommes plus chez nous. Maintenant les gens m'ont téléphoné. Et ce sont des
gens qui n'ont pas la possibilité de payer une boule d'*akassa*, sans la
participation d'autres. Donc on a profité de ça la. Et ils sont combien de
personnes, nous nous sommes partis retirer de l'église catholique.

[but someone is practicing his religion, the woman is in trance and the priest
over there he sends people. They took her and destroyed her the pearls, the instruments of Vodun that the woman has. It means that we are no longer in our
home and people have called me. And these are people who cannot even pay
for a bowl of *akassa* without the participation of others. So, they took advan-
tage of that. And with other people we went to the Catholic Church to take
them.]

Confrontation follows as the Daah leaves accompanied by others to reclaim
what to him and to the others are sacred articles taken from the woman. He offers this event as further evidence of modern domination by Christians, the per-
sisting devaluation of local religious tradition and their outcome in the separation of families—in this case the extended family.

Or c'est une somme chez eux. Le père est d'accord pour son enfant, la mère est
d'accord mais vous vous avez dit qu'on ne doit pas réaliser ce truc, cette chose
du diable et vous êtes parti. De quel droit vous usez lorsque moi je suis
d'accord? Ma femme est d'accord, il n'y a pas de problème. L'enfant est
d'accord.

[items taken] is a large amount of money for them. The father agrees, the
mother agrees but you have said that this thing cannot happen, this thing of the
devil and you leave. What right have you when I agree with it? My wife agrees,
there is no problem, the child agrees]

While at the macro (state) level, religions seem to coexist peacefully, peaceful
coexistence does not roll to the micro where interreligious marriages are a
source of stress. Take the following example where a man who is Catholic attempts to impose his will on non Christian members of the nuclear family.

Toi le mari qui n'a même pas doté la fille et tu es catholique, tu es parti retirer
l'enfant avec bâton et tout, vous lui avez détruit les accoutrements. . . . Quelle
collaboration nous pouvons faire en ce moment-là?

[You the husband who has not even paid a dowry and you are Catholic, and
you take the child[38] with a stick and everything and you destroyed the items . . .
What collaboration can we do now?]

Notice the Daah's stress on the absent dowry, pointing to its cultural significance and in this case a disregard for and deviation from the expected. This de-

parture from the norm should lessen the man's marital and parental rights. This case shows a lack of respect for tradition, an attitude of superiority on the part of this man and the tensions ensuing. As an additional example of friction between religious practices, the Daah also describes his difficult relationship with his brother-Catholic-priest whom he says he loves and accepts unconditionally despite the brother's indifference.

Or moi j'accepte que mon frère, j'ai un frère qui est prêtre jusqu'à l'heure ou nous parlons. On l'appelle [donne le nom]. . . Il est prêtre catholique . . . lorsque moi je voulais organiser quelque chose dans le village, il n'a pas mis pied là, il n'a pas mis pied là. Alors ça là c'est gênant . . . et c'est à cause de l'argent de la religion traditionnelle que l'on a utilisé pour que lui il fréquente pour devenir prêtre. . . . J'ai essayé de le voir, il a fui. Quel enseignement il a eu et aujourd'hui il ne peut plus participer à sa religion? Je vous dis . . . posez-moi toutes questions moi je vais répondre, et je veux être identifié parce que moi je ne mens pas. . . .Celui-là c'est un frère. Je dis bien que c'est un frère. Mais lorsqu'il est ordonné, tout le village nous avons participé. . . . Il y a quelqu'un même qui a payé pour une voiture. Mais depuis que lui il est ordonné il n'a jamais mis pied dans la maison.

[And me, I accept that my brother, I have a brother who is a priest even as we speak. His name I [gives name] . . . He is Catholic priest. When I tried to organize something in the village, he did not step foot there. So that is embarrassing. And it is because of the money of traditional religion that has been used for him to become priest. . . . I tried to see him but he fled. . . . What teachings has he had today that he can no longer participate in his religion? . . . am telling you . . . ask me all questions me, I am going to respond, and I what to be identified because I am not lying. . . . That one is a brother. . . I am indeed saying he is a brother. But when he was ordained, all the village participated. There is even someone who paid for a car. But since his ordination he has never step foot in the house.]

I suggested to the respondent his brother might be afraid, given all that fictive inventiveness about Vodun and accurate or not Vodun's association with sorcery and satanism in the western world. However, he did not find fear a likely reason for his brother or any priest to stay away from kin. So he asked me,

Peur de quoi? Moi je lui ai donné ma garantie; il dit, 'je veux construire.' Je lui dis, 'je te donne une parcelle et je vais surveiller.' D'abord si tu es avec Dieu, tu as peur du diable, ça veut dire qu'il y a quelque chose qui ne marche pas. Tu es avec Yayi Boni et tu as peur du Ministre de l'Intérieur? Non, tu ne peux avoir peur du Ministre de l'Intérieur puisque le Ministre de l'Intérieur est sous Yayi Boni, mais c'est Dieu qui gouverne tout. Moi je n'ai pas peur d'eux. Je m'en vais dans l'église. Pourquoi moi je n'ai pas peur? Si un Pasteur m'invite moi je me présente. . . . Donc voilà.

[Fear of what? I gave him my guarantee; he says 'I want to build' and I tell him ' I am giving him a piece of land and I will look after it.' First of all if you

are with God, and you are afraid of the Devil something is not working. You
are with Yayi Boni and you are afraid of the Minister of the Interior? No, you
cannot be afraid of the Minister of the Interior since the Minister of the Interior
is under Yayi Boni. But God governs everything. First of all if you are with
God, you are afraid of the devil, it means that something is not working. Me I
am not afraid of them, I go to the Church. Why am I not afraid? If a pastor invites me I am present. . . . So there it is.]

Interesting parallel. Harvard-educated economist Dr. Boni Yayi is the country's
President. The Daah's choice of comparison implies his Catholic brother-priest
stays away because despite being priest, his faith lacks strength. Of course, an
interview with the brother would have made the discussion strong and enthrall-
ing. Despite knowing his name, Daah's brother could not be located.

Whether or not the Daah correctly perceives the reasons for his brother's
distance from family, this perception is consistent with his view expressed earlier that religious coexistence characteristic of the small nation is not as peaceful
as first appears despite national days to celebrate officially different affiliations—January 10 for Vodou, other special days for Muslims, still others for
Christians—as if each faith were well respected with equal rights in the society.
If not outright anger, there are hurts and resentments simmering, consequence of
the religious plurality and of tensions at the micro levels. Thus, while Benin is
known as a religious democracy, when this and other respondents communicate
family tensions, result of coexistence, it does appear that state level democracy
has not trickled down deeply enough into the daily experiences of the people.

> Tout à fait, et ce n'est pas le catholicisme seulement, les sectes-la, c'est tous les
> sectes-la qui servent à séparer les familles. Je vais vous dire quelque chose
> puisque tout ce que je vais dire c'est vérifiable. Nous sommes en Afrique,
> précisément au Bénin. Qui peut oser parler des Musulmans ici au Bénin?
> Personne. Tout de suite on va t'attaquer. . . . Lorsque . . . Benoît XVI a parlé
> des Musulmans, vous avez le bruit qui a couru dans tout le monde. . . . Ici au
> Bénin, si quelqu'un critique ouvertement la religion Catholique il va avoir des
> problèmes. Mais quand on critique ouvertement notre culture, personne ne dit
> mot.

> [Exactly, and that is not Catholicism only, those sects, it is all the sects those
> that serve to separate families. I am going to say something because all I am
> going to say is verifiable. We are in Africa, precisely in Benin. Who dares to
> speak of Muslims here in Benin? Nobody. Immediately you will be attacked.
> When Benoit XVI spoke of Muslims, you have the noise that shook the world.
> Here in Benin, if someone openly critics the Catholic religion there will be
> problems. But when one openly critics our culture, no one says a word]

What the respondent is expressing is his perception of an existing stratification
where traditional religion lacks power relative to others in the society because it
is openly and unfairly denigrated, condemned and dominated. Hence traditional
religion has become a stranger at home. The view also sheds light on the attitude

of the "run away" brother-priest whose silence appears to his sibling assimilation into the other side and unspoken critique of traditional religion. Note too in this quote how the respondent interchanges Vodun religion and Vodou culture. From this viewpoint, Vodun religion is Beninese culture.

Despite the double vision of the world and potential for strain and splits inside nuclear and extended families, the influence of tradition is clearly felt as in the couple who consulted their priest after pressures from kin to seek traditional help for infertility in a society where a barren has reduced value. In fact, it is precisely because of the meeting of two visions that family's influence on members can best be assessed. In such a setting, when a member claims a single vision mostly or completely empty of tradition, family steps in and conflicts may ensue. Additional statements regarding the importance of being rooted in a family, and family's influence on members follow:

> Quand on te dit de laisser ta tradition, même si vous êtes catholique, si vous êtes Pasteur, vous êtes né dans une famille, vous avez une origine. Exactement comme le Seigneur Jésus christ, il est né dans une famille donc il a fait la tradition, c'est la tradition, c'est dans sa famille. Il a pris les formes de la tradition de sa famille et il a amené tout ça [inaudible] qui est devenu la religion catholique plus tard. Ce n'est pas lui qui a créé la religion Catholique.

> [When they tell you to leave your tradition, even if you are Catholic, if you are Pastor, you are born in a family, you have an origin. Exactly like Jesus Christ, who was born in a family so he had a tradition, it is in his family. He took the forms of the tradition of his family, and made it what later became Catholicism. He did not create the Catholic religion.]

Thus family's significant impact on the everyday life of the people of Benin and West Africa is important to stress.

> Vous savez, [inaudible] l'Afrique en général, ceux qui se disent aujourd'hui catholique, musulmans, chrétiens en général sont des gens qui viennent d'une famille.. . . d'une famille. . . béninoise donc traditionaliste. Donc de temps en temps, eux, ils retournent. . . . Ils retournent à leur tradition. Donc, c'est le cas général ça. Mais . . . il y a des gens qui après avoir échoué dans d'autres religions ils reviennent voir. Par exemple, . . . ils doivent avoir une maladie . . . elles n'ont pas d'enfants, elles ne peuvent pas concevoir, ils n'ont pas de travail, ils sont rentrés dans les religions . . . les religions-la . . . les sectes. Bon, on prie, on prie, on prie. Donc tu pries pendant cinq ans et ce que tu demandes n'arrive pas, tu es obligé de te retrouver encore. . . . La différence chez moi c'est que je ne vous impose pas.

> [You know . . . Africa in general, those who say today Catholics, Muslims, Christians in general are people who have come from a family . . . Beninese . . . so, traditionalist. So from time to time, they return, they return to their tradition. So that is the case in general. But . . . there are people who after having failed with other religions come see me. For example . . . they have an illness . . . they don't have children, they cannot conceive, they do not have work, they have

converted to other religions . . . those religions . . . the sects. So this in general
is the case. . . . Hence they pray, and pray and pray. So you pray for five years
and what you are asking for does not come to you, you have to find] yourself
again. The difference with me is that I do not impose.

Finding oneself means returning to family roots, the ancestral generations,
the ancestral religion. Beninese people are strongly influenced by generations of
extended family. Family prevails. Tradition matters.

Family: Haitian Americans and African Americans.

For Haitian Americans, family's interference and influence on the retention or
rejection of religious practices will be different from the Beninese. Though Haitians in Haiti and possibly first generation Haitian Americans behave at least in
some ways as the Beninese, the ethnogenesis of Haitians developed differently.
Given the initial geographic and cultural seclusion following the thirteen year
Revolutionary War combined with a series of unique historico-political circumstances, Haiti's popular Catholicism will contain some elements transported
from Africa but transformed from the original forms and content (see Métraux,
1958; Desmangles, 1992). For example in Haiti, the historical *lakou* was much
like what can still be found in some Beninese villages (Métraux 1958; Desmangles, 1992). But even in rural Haiti this structure is fading, and it is non-existent
in urban areas where the nuclear family forms prevail (see Métraux, 1958). In
Haiti, the influence of generations on the individual is less. Traditional elements
were transformed over the years through geographical isolation, the interpen-
etration of foreign cultures (including the United States) and the on-going influence of Protestant sects (also current reality in Benin).

The ethnogenesis of Haitian Americans also develops differently from the
Haitian. First generation Haitian Americans especially educated outside the
homeland will be influenced less by African ancestry and family with regards to
religion and religious practice. Even more pronounced will be distancing from
ancestry and family for the second generation Americans. The younger these
Americans, the more time and interactions within the American land, the farther
removed from the influence of generation, the lesser the impact of African traditions.

The scholar Patrick Bellegarde-Smith provides a good illustration. In an interview with Krista Tippet, he acknowledges Tippet's statement that his grandfather, Dantès Bellegarde, was "a great philosopher and statesman in Haitian
history . . . an intellectual who said that Vodou was primitive, that Christianity
was superior." But Bellegarde-Smith, university Professor and *houngan asogwé*,
added the following to Tippet's statement (Tippet and Bellegarde-Smith, 2008:
156).

I was very, very close to my grandfather growing up. I benefited from his library in his home in Port-au-Prince. . . . And people are telling me, 'Well, he

must be spinning in his grave.' Not at all. He's quite satisfied that I'm making amends for him, for the kinds of things he refused to recognize. He also thought that anything having to do with Africa was no good, all the way down to his kinky, nappy hair. Well, I'm proud of my nappy hair. I'm nappy-headed, and so was he. He was pro-French, of a family that was light-skinned, had been light-skinned for a number of generations, and would have make very, very sure that the entire family for generations to come would stay light-skinned, because we're not going back to Africa because that is savagery. Well, Africa does not mean that to me at all.

When I wanted to get my mother angry as a child, I would say, 'Mother I love them drums.' And she would say to me, 'Oh god, why can't you like the violin? The violin is much better.' But when she was on her deathbed, I would put on some Haitian music. Days before her death, she was moving to the tune of Haitian drums.

Bellegarde-Smith adopted a different path from that traced by mother and grandfather. Closeness to family did not influence his choice of religious practice after he had lived in the United States.

Another example of the reduced impact of family in the choices of Haitian Americans is the case of my own sister, Marie-Claude Rigaud, a more than four-decade-long immigrant to the United States and staunch Catholic with whom I discussed this issue (2009). Here what she had to say:

I cannot miss a Sunday Mass without feeling guilty about it. My husband André and I have six children, five who were born in the United States. All received a Catholic education from elementary school to the University level. Yet, only two have followed the religious path that was set for them by us, their parents. And one of the two does not practice Catholicism. That only leaves one.

Though family networks are alive and first generation Haitian immigrants stay connected with kin across the Atlantic, though many these immigrants adhere to normative expectations of sending money back home, transnational family links seem more for the purpose of economic support than emotional attachment. Haitian American connections with kin, especially elders on the other side of the Atlantic, may be due to a strong sense of economic responsibility developed during socialization. But too other reasons for these transnational connections may be historical pride, the hope of returning someday to the motherland, not wanting to completely give up that cherished dream of going back even if at times returning may seem an impossible dream. Sending money to Haiti also preserves the collective memory and identity so often transmitted to younger generations of Haitian Americans who may have never visited the country (see Waters, 1992).

Hence the influence of family evident in the Beninese context will be much less, or even absent in the Haitian American. The religious choices of Haitian Americans will be influenced more by non-familial or fictive kin relationships in their immediate environments abroad, than by intimate connections with the extended family in the United States or across the Atlantic. Reduced or lack of family (generational) influence represents a major difference between the Haitian American and Beninese contexts. Data on this influence of family on the religious choice or other practice of Beninese Americans and other West African immigrants to the United States would further strengthen this analysis.

At the opening of this work, we heard from a Vodun religious professional on the necessity of Vodun schools. If these schools were developed in both Benin and Haiti and the children of these nations required to attend, the new educational system might lead more and more to a shift in the direction of local culture, greater attachment to ancestry and extended family, a more pronounced double belonging and, to the extent it still remains a reshaping of Catholicism with deeper marks of local traditions. But even without these schools, family influence is already strong in Benin. Given the ancestral nature of Vodun religion and culture, such schools would only reinforce this influence of family traditions. Haitian Americans originating from such a school setting might be more inclined to double belong or syncretize their religious beliefs and as a consequence rely more on, and be influenced more by, family dictates. But these are only *ifs*, because so far Vodun schools are a dream that the Vodun hierarchy is hoping will become reality. It is not reality in Benin. It is not reality in Haiti. Family's influence on religious choices is one factor that separates Haitians and Haitian Americans from the Beninese. In both nations, it is the strength of family influence in daily life that Vodun formal education would increase.

An analogy might be the recent rise of Haitian Creole next to French as official language of Haiti, consequently the use of Creole in the school context. In their interactions with each other in the United States, Haitian Americans originating from such a linguistic setting will more likely continue using both languages, more so than Americans who grew up in Haiti when French alone, at that time sign of education and status, was the official mode of communication while Creole was devalued, stigmatized and prohibited especially in school settings. As one social scientist puts it: "the conflict and divisions of the colonial slave past continue to plague Haitians in their new conditions of exile" (Buchanan, 1979, 310). The point being made is that issues of class associated with French and Creole continue outside of Haiti in the Haitian immigrant context.

Speaking of French and Creole, Haitian Archbishop Guy Sansaricq puts it this way (St. Jean, 2008: 170).

> Language preference depends on the social class. Haitians speak Creole in Haiti. There is a percentage fluent in French. In the U.S., Haitians who are better educated move in neighborhoods where there are no Haitians. In Haiti, there is a great evolution toward Creole. So Haitians who have been [in the U.S.] 20 years have not gone through the transition process. In every group there is a certain [segment] where some prefer to assimilate to mainstream culture. The Haitian community is not monolithic. Some people hang on to French, but the majority is the Creole.

Given the current discussion about religion and to test the fit of the linguistic analogy, one might attempt replacing 'language' with 'religion' in the Bishop's statement. The substitution is italicized; see what that does.

> *Religious* preference depends on social class. In the United States, better educated Haitians move in neighborhoods where there are no Haitians. In Haiti there is a great evolution toward *Vodun*. So Haitians who have been [in the U.S.] 20 years have not gone through the transition process. In every group, there is a certain segment where some prefer to assimilate to mainstream culture. The Haitian community is not monolithic. Some people hang on to *Catholicism*, but the majority is the *Vodun*.

'Nicely done,' one might say, except the substitution of religion for language does not seem to work quite as well. And the Bishop-author whose approval was not sought before substitution may not agree with the new meaning. There are indeed differences between the importation of language and that of religion in a statement, but especially in real life.

The possible introduction of Vodun schools in Haiti would indeed bring Haitians and Haitian Americans originating from such setting closer to the Beninese, since Vodun, ancestral religion practiced in the family is likely to increase family's influence on members. This is not the case for Creole, spoken in Haiti inside and outside the family setting. Moreover, while Creole is often associated with primarily monolingual masses, the ability to speak it transcends class and religious affiliations. One hundred percent Haitians speak Creole. Furthermore, in Christian contexts inside and outside of Haiti, Creole does not carry the stigma associated with the practice of Vodun (although, more and more inside and outside Haiti, Vodun is being seen for what it is, a popular religion and way of life originated in West Africa). Moreover, it is not likely that Creole would increase the influence of family members on the religious choices of members.

So far the discussion has focused on the Beninese, the Haitian and Haitian American, their similarities and differences. But what about African Americans? My observations and interviews in Benin suggest the Beninese think of Haitians as *alter ego*, or perhaps as their twins, and African Americans as brothers and sisters. Many informants say their children marrying an African American would be an honor. They describe this marriage as recapturing the past to find a long lost relative. Most think of Africa America as an extension of the African land. The Beninese show pride in the economic success of diaspora Africans including the African Americans. They point especially to those who returned from Brazil, most living on the coastal region in the city of Ouidah. They inform also on others who returned to the West African land, like the JAH family previously of the island of Guadeloupe. The Beninese wish to see more of these Americans, and United States brothers and sisters, in the land of origin. Still, cultural connections of African Americans with Benin specifically are more dif-

ficult to establish than for Haitian Americans, many who are determined to retain a Haitian identity that contains strong elements of the West African.

While both Haitian Americans and African Americans have African ancestry, it seems Haitians and Haitian Americans are closer to West Africa than African Americans. The Haitian imagination, which includes the Catholic sacramental closely resembles the Beninese sacramental imagination (see
Desmangles, 1992). But the Haitian American imagination and Haitian American Catholic imagination, still rooted in the West African, may hold a permu-
tated character.

Though not initiates of Vodun religion, the self identified Catholic Haitian
Americans interviewed in the mid-2000 Midwest seem either to carry marks of a
Haitian culture of Vodun, or are aware of such marks in the Haitian American
(see Desmangles, 1992; Greggus, 1994). As one respondent put it (see Shaw-
Taylor and Tuch, 2008: 168-169).

> Whether the Haitian wants to accept . . . it or not, our belief system is very
> strongly affected by our folklore. In fact, I was thinking about that last night.
> Last night, coming back from a party, I was crossing—what's the name of that
> street—where they have cemeteries on both sides of the street . . . And I said to
> myself, "If I tell a Haitian that I was crossing that thing and I saw a dead per-
> son, a zombie, crossing the street, 60 percent of Haitians will not challenge
> what I say." They will accept the possibility that a zombie could be crossing the
> street. And the same Haitian, who is a devout Catholic . . . devout Catholic. But
> if I tell them that I saw a zombie crossing the street, there is something in the
> back of their mind that could suggest that that could be true.

> Some Haitians . . . will tell you that Vodou is a religion and I believe it is. I be-
> lieve Vodou is a religion because it's a set of beliefs for the majority of Haitians
> . . . the people, the peasants, you know, the [prolétaire]. You have 75 to 80 per-
> cent or maybe more than that . . . in Haiti. And most of them believe in Vodou.
> But is . . . superstition the backbone of Vodouism or which one comes first? . . .
> To me I put them in the same basket. Maybe I do that for lack of knowledge or
> ignorance but to me that's the same thing. Is superstition . . . supposed to be a
> tenet of Vodouism or is Vodouism? . . . None of them is Catholic and that's
> what makes the Catholicism, as practiced by the Haitians. That makes it imper-
> fect, somewhat adulterated, because it is tainted by that fundamental knowledge
> in the culture, that fundamental nature of the culture, that fundamental element.
> . . . I know I was joking when I say that I saw that zombie crossing the street,
> you know, theoretically. . . . This is a pure invention, a pure lie, but a lot of
> Haitians might say, "You never know." *This* is Catholic. *Thi*s is . . . Haitian.
> You . . . never know because, Dèyè Mon, Gin Mon [beyond mountains there
> are mountains]. That is part of the mystery of things.

Catholic Bishop Guy Sansaricq who disagrees with this assessment re-
sponds (St. Jean, 2008: 172).

> This is speculation—not scientific observation. It is based on personal observa-
> tion that needs to be tested. Vodou has permeated Haitian culture to a vast de-

gree and that is a fact, but the Church has always stressed the difference between Catholicism and Vodou. In a country where education is not advanced
many marginal Catholics accept a number of the tenets of Vodou religion, well-
educated Haitians have nothing to do with Vodou.

The Catholic Church in Benin also stresses the difference even as boundaries are
fluid, thus lines of separations unclear. The Bishop does admit however that
"Vodou has permeated Haitian culture." And that statement is important for our
discussion of a religious connection with Benin and the nature of the sacramental imagination in these populations. Vodun is evident in the culture and in cultural elements including songs that Haitians continue singing long after having
left for different shores, long after forgotting their French. When Haitians have
forgotten everything, Creole remains in the mind, and so do folk songs carrying
the names of deities, rhythms and other marks of Vodun.

Popular and sacred songs are important. "Possibly the most important me-
diums for transmitting information are rituals and oral traditions such as myths,
songs, legends, or prayers" (Barnes 1989: 8). Haitians sing the popular folkloric
song about *Papa Gédé*, handsome, dressed in white, ready to walk the steps of
the national palace. The song is one of many in the cultural toolbox. I heard it on
the radio, when attending concerts, and so did everyone else. People sang (sing)
this and other songs without knowing, thinking much about or questioning the
broader meaning. But who is *Papa Gédé*? Edna Bay (2001) explains,

> Ghédé has been preserved in Haitian Vodou and . . . derives from
> Ghédévi (literally, children of Ghédé), the people said to have been the
> original inhabitants of the Abomey plateau who opposed the founders
> of Dahomey and were displaced and presumably sold.

Of course, there are many other such signs of the culturalization of Vodou in
Haiti's songs. There are songs about *Erzulie Fréda* and other deities, songs that
use the term *Simbi*, but songs for many have lost their traditional religious meaning. They have become part of the cultural toolbox. The Haitian sings this music
without necessarily double belonging, a clear indication of the inculturation
(culturalization) of Vodou.

Marks of West African tradition do not appear strong in the African
American Catholic respondents interviewed in the Midwest due at least in part
to a Protestant influenced Catholicism. As one African American researcher
writes, in the African American Catholic community, spirituality is

> [c]oncern . . . with the desire of the African American community to know it-
> self and to know God in the context of African American experience, history
> and culture, [a concern] as old as the first sermon preached by enslaved Afri-
> cans and their brothers and sisters huddled together in some plantation swamp,
> and as new as the reflections of James Cone . . . and others beginning in the
> 1960s. It is a theology of, about, and by African Americans. And while the
> formal proponents of this theology were a group of creative Protestant scholars,

African American Catholic thinkers have used it as a point of departure to
elaborate theological reflection that is both African American and Catholic. . . .
The African American bishops, in their pastoral letter, What We Have Seen and
Heard, spoke eloquently of some of the qualities of an African spirituality
(Kelly 2000, 377-78).

A Protestant influence means less focus on the sacramental or the idea of representation and divine-in-the-world. It also means a prevailing dialectical imagination and fewer similarities with Vodun. The Evangelicals interviewed in Benin
wanted nothing to do with Vodou. Rather, they wanted to "Let God be God"
which corresponds to the dialectical view of Protestant theologians (see Tracy,
1981). It seems thus, the near absence of Vodou in the culture or, more accurately, the near absent focus on its presence may have to do more with Protestant
influences on the education and the everyday life of generations of African
Americans. "African religions did not survive in happenstance fragments in the
New World. They blended, shifted, and took on new forms in response to new
social conditions, and they continue to do so today" (Barnes, 1989: 87). The
apparent disruption seems at least in part due to a lack of compatibility between
two religious practices, and the impact of a Protestant offshoot on the ethnogenesis of African Americans.

I strongly disagree with E. Franklin Frazier when he writes that

> probably never before in history has a people been so completely stripped of its
> social heritage as the Negroes who were brought to America. Other conquered
> races have continued to worship their household gods within the intimate circle
> of their kinsmen. But American slavery destroyed household gods and dis-
> solved the bonds of sympathy and affection between men of the same blood
> and household. Old men and women might have brooded over memories of
> their African homeland, but they could not change the world about them.
> Through force of circumstances, they had to acquire a new language, adopt new
> habits of labor, and take over, however imperfectly, the folkways of the Ameri-
> can environment. Their children who knew only the American environment,
> soon forgot the few memories that had been passed onto them and developed
> motivations and modes of behavior in harmony with the new world. They chil-
> dren's children have often recalled with skepticism the fragments of stories
> concerning Africa which have been preserved in their families. But, of the hab-
> its and customs as well as the hope s and fears that characterized the life of
> their forebearers in Africa, nothing remains. When educated Negroes of the
> present generation attempt to resurrect the forgotten memories of their ances-
> tors, they are seeking in the alien culture of Africa a basis for race pride and ra-
> cial identification. Hence, when a young sophisticated Negro poet asks,
>   What is Africa to me?
> And answers with true poetic license that the African heritage surges up in him
>   In an old remembered way
> we hear the voice of a new race consciousness in a world of conflict and frus-
> tration rather than the past speaking through traditions that have become re-

fined and hallowed as they have been transmitted from generation to generation (Frazier 1939, 21-22).

Similar such ideas can be found also in Frazier's The Negro Church in America (1963: 1), where he states:

> In studying any phase of the character and development of the social and cultural life of the Negro in the United States, one must recognize from the beginning that because of the manner in which the Negroes were captured in Africa and enslaved, they were practically stripped of their social heritage.

In the *Souls of Black Folk*, W.E.B. DuBois demonstrates the link with the past, especially in sacred songs. Other authors too have written about the importance of the African American Church as retention, a "most characteristic expression of African character" and "a continuation of the slave church which invented and integrated sociocultural components: the preacher, the music, and the 'frenzy'" (Green and Driver 1978: 197). This important retention is also discussed in more recent writings (see among others Slevin and Wingrove, 1998). And while Herkovits finds fewer retentions than are present in other enslaved populations, he is not as extreme as Frazier (see Frazier 1963: endnote 1 page 1).

Some reasons offered by Frazier (1963: 2) for the "stripped . . . social heritage" are plantation size which, according to him, had an "influence on the nature of contact between slaves and whites." Where plantations were large, interaction between enslaved and slavemaster was reduced which made it easier for the enslaved to maintain their culture.

On small plantations, the enslaved took on the religion of the masters. "All this tended to bring about as completely as possible a loss of the Negro's African cultural heritage" (1963: 3). However, Frazier does not take into account the introduction of a dialectical imagination in this population, an imagination which has little compatibility with the sacramental or with Vodou. As several authors point out (including Métraux) those who want to abandon traditional religion find refuge in Protestant Christianity where they cannot be touched or punished by gods they previously worshipped. Protestantism offers proctection from deities. There also seem many contradictions in the thought of Frazier, for example when he writes: "One of the best sources of information on the manner in which the negro adapted Christianity to this peculiar psychological and social needs is to be found in that great body of sacred folk music known as 'Negro Sprituals.'" (1963: 12). It seems these sacred songs would be signs of continuity which elsewhere he denies exist. Referring to the Spirituals, Frazier also writes

> From the standpoint of his early condition, the negro was constantly concerned with death. . . . For the slave death was an everpresent and-compelling fact 'because of the cheapness with his life was regarded. The slave was a tool, a thing, a utility, a commodity, he was faced constantly with the eminent threat of death, of which the terrible overseer

was a symbol; and the awareness that he (the slave) was only chattel property" (1963, 13-14).

My own analysis of preferred sacred songs in Benin (Quénum and St. Jean, 2008) suggests death a constant theme. The theme of death in negro spirituals too may be retention from an original culture. Frazier failed to peel the many layers of the ethnogenesis of African Americans.

Several important areas where research might yield tight connections between the Beninese, the Haitian American and the African American is the deep respect for elders in all these traditions. Also needing more research is respect for the dead, evident in the lavishness of funerals, the importance of female virginity before marriage (see Slevin and Wingrove), the sister-brother fictive kinships, the use of the body in religious worship including the African American Catholic.

Catholic or not, African Americans are diverse. While Vodun culture does not appear to have permeated African American culture to the extent that it has the Haitian, New Orleans with its larger Catholic population and likely dominant sacramental imagination may tell a different story about the African American religious imagination. After the Haitian revolution, many freedmen fled to New Orleans looking for safety (Fandrich 2008: 188). "The Haitian traditions blended in the city's underground with Cuban, African and local black Creole Voodoo lines"[39] (Frandrich 2008: 189). In other words, the New Orleans sacramental imagination may help discover the missing link between Beninese, Haitians, Haitian Americans, and African Americans.

Interesting and useful to this research would be to discover if second and third generation Haitian Americans without tight familial connections in Haiti withheld the original collective memory or have become "protestantized," more dialectical in their religious imaginations. If anything, what would Benin, and Allada (home of Toussaint L'ouverture) mean to them?

Summary and Conclusion

Anselm Strauss (1978: 5-6) writes "the negotiated order on any given day could be conceived as the sum total of the organization's rules and policies, along with whatever agreements, understandings, pacts, contracts, and other working arrangements currently obtained." Strauss believed even the most restrictive contexts must negotiate to survive. Strauss' ideas are applicable to the present study.

In the preceeding pages, some adepts of Catholicism and Vodun share their insights on religious coexistence in multiethnic Benin.[40] The extended family (generation) plays a major role in the negotiation of religious borders and eventual ethnogenesis. The outcome of negotiations vary from double belonging (syncretism) to various forms of inculturation.

The Catholic imagination is dynamic. More porous than the Protestant, it absorbs the surrounding culture and transforms itself (or is transformed) into multiple catholic imaginations.

The Catholic imagination absorbs Beninese culture and seems at ease with Vodun. But there are limits to Catholic imagination's porosity. The Catholic imagination accepts positive Vodun (the intuition of Mawu or God) and Vodun culture. The Catholic imagination rejects the Vodun system.

The face of the Catholic imagination varies with the level of societal development. While in modern United States it may appear ritualized,[41] protestantized, it is spirited and vodun-ized in West Africa. The Catholic imagination begins where the people are, at a particular time and place. As negotiations proceed, it increasingly sheds the incompatible to birth an inculturated form. The more traditional a society and influential its family system, the greater the impact of tradition on the Catholic imagination and the more syncretic its ethnogenesis outcome.

Catholic imaginations vary on the basis of historical, generational, educational experience. Catholic imaginations vary on the basis of ethnicity.

Though the Catholic imagination is less open to diversity than Vodun, the Catholic imagination holds a close second place. Evangelicals and Muslims appear least open to diversity.

Catholic imaginations contribute to and move toward (but in some cases, away from) the broader Catholic imagination.

Rooted in local culture, each catholic imagination is an effective tool for the study of variations in preferences between catholic and non Catholic originating from the same culture. We would expect more cultural similarities between groups originated from the same culture who also share a Catholic imagination.

Each catholic imagination helps to define more sharply the contours of the broader Catholic imagination.

The Catholic imagination can serve as ideal-type and effective tool for the comparative study of such issues as social justice, religious diversity, and what ties the West African to the African diaspora.

Twa fey, twa racine [three leaves, three roots], *jété blié, ranmassé songé* [throw out, forget; collect, remember]. Some things must not be discarded, insist the lyrics of this Haitian Creole song. If not used, like roots and leaves they must be gathered and preserved. So is the family, mirror of ancestry, generation, and repository of tradition. As forced immigration and other historical disruptions permute generational links so too do they redirect the traditional lines connecting past, present and future generations. The direction of ethnogenesis is the outcome of constant negotiations.

Future research should assess negotiations more carefully to determine, outside of family pressures, what drives the choice of a particular religious practice. How is the choice negotiated? Given family pressures, why do some people double-belong and others inculturate? The work of the sociologist Rodney Stark would help this analysis (see Stark and Finke, 2000).

The Catholic imagination is a sociological "unmarked," useful in explaining not only negotiated religious spaces, but also everyday behaviors and differences among ethnic populations. Borrowing from Wayne Brekhus' "A Sociology of the Unmarked" it may be time for sociologists to "redirect our focus" to this unmarked, yet potent tool for analysis.

***

On June 30, 2008, as I boarded an Air France flight, I gave a final look to the airport whose name had recently changed to *Aéroport International Cardinal Bernardin Gantin* to honor the memory of the late Cardinal. My work seemed unfinished. But research is never done. This study has only scratched the surface of an important issue. Additional inquiry is needed on the link between the Catholic imagination and social justice, the issue of similarities and difference between people of the African diaspora, and a host of other issues that surface in the interviews.

Notes

1. This research was made possible by a two-year lecture/research grant from the Fulbright scholar program.

2. I am using the *Daah* title (used to address Vodun priest) for this respondent on a much higher level in the hierarchy. His exact title is not revealed because of issues of confidentiality and the possibility that he might recognized.

3. I prefer 'secular' to 'profane.'

4. The quote in French is in its original publication. Whenever possible, I provide the French version in addition to its English translation.

5. See David Tracy's *The Analogical Imagination.*

6. Personal communication with Beninese priest André Quénum.

7. Interestingly in Bénin there is a tree named *Bois Caïman.*

8. Sociologists of religion recognize the role of *Bois Caïman* for social integration. For literature on this issue see Jean Fils-Aimé's *Vodou Je me Souviens.*

9. Thanks to Dr. Worden for this note.

10. I use the word "impact" despite objections from Dr. Valerie Hunt, who suggests instead "influence," "affect," or "effect." This preference represents a long standing debate between Dr. Hunt and colleague Dr. Ania Zajicek, both sociologists at the University of Arkansas Fayetteville.

11. Several respondents reacted negatively to the term animism which they say was given by colonizers.

12. In Benin, "Catholicisme Vécu" was a favorite title for this work. Several respondents expressed their dislike for "Catholic imagination.'

13. This statement has been attributed to more than one author including the Reverend Dr. Martin Luther King.

14. I am using "openness to other" instead of "social equality." The literature points to interracial marriage as an indicator of social equality. But thinking further, one recognizes that openness is a more accurate term. If interracial marriage occur between partners of the same social class, it is less an indicator of social equality than openness to racial equality. Social equality is too broad a concept to be used here. I thank Ania Zajicek whose question about the relevance of the concept provoked this further thinking.

15. If the word existed—it does not—the *este* in *évêque-este* indicates the feminine version of 'bishop.' As of now, there are no women priests in the Catholic Church. This comment by a priest with a wonderful sense of humor was meant to provoke laughter.

16. Opinions on this differs.

17. Originally, *amiyo* was a dish offered to divinities during Vaudou ceremonies. Today, it is enjoyed by everyone regardless of religious appartenance.

18. My emphasis. This is one example of European perception of Africans.

19. A statistical table can be found in the index. Thanks to the Archdiocese of Cotonou for this important information.

20. Term used by Greeley in his *Catholic Imagination* (2000) to describe an array of sacramentals in the Catholic Church.

21. Kinkpon, R. P. Philippe, "The family in Africa: values, hopes and threats." *La Croix du Bénin*, May, 2007.

22. *Cradle Catholic* refers to people who were born in Catholicism.

23. See Feagin and Sikes'1994 *Living with Racism: The Black Middle Class Experience.*

24. "Once a Catholic, always a Catholic" says Andrew Greeley. Cultural Catholics are baptized, identify with the Catholic Church, but do not practice regularly.

25. *Yovo* is a *fon-gbe* word which most often means "white," but is also used to refer to a foreigner, or something foreign.

26. See *Le Sillon Noir S'Éxplique*, 1998, No. 13.

27. http://cat.inist.fr/?aModele=afficheN&cpsidt=12053497

28. See Greeley, Andrew; see also Feagin and Feagin, *Racial and Ethnic Relations*.

29. Author's translation.

30. Though syncretism and inculturation may be consequences.

31. Of Protestantism, Maya Deren writes that it "has been able to insist more clearly, upon its incompatibility with Vodoun. Indeed to the Vodoun serviteurs, there is a far greater incompatibility between the two branches of Christianity than there is between Catholics and themselves."

32. It may be that they are aware of what Leslie Desmangles writing about Haiti refers to as *symbiosis*. The use of Catholic Saints to represent Vodou deities (see also Maya Deren).

33. "Any attempt to account for the changes that African religious system underwent in the New World must be sensitive to the complex interactions between memory and the material conditions of life in that new place" (Brown, 1989).

34. http://www.webster.edu/~corbetre/haiti/haiti.html

35. *Hayti* was the name given to the island by its Indian original population.

36. http://www.webster.edu/~corbetre/haiti/haiti.html

37. On the issue of Catholicism and Vodun in Haiti, the work of Leslie Desmangles holds useful information about what he calls *symbiosis*.

38. It is not clear if the respondent is referring to the man's child or to his wife even as he uses 'enfant' which means "child." This is suggested because 'child' could be emphasizing the fact that this is a younger woman. Of course this language would seem sexist in the United States but is not unusual in this case and has no sexist undertone.

39. See more interesting details in Fandrich's 2008 essay.

40. I thank Dr. Steven Worden for the idea of negotiated order.

41. I thank Dr. André Rigaud for that idea.

APPENDIXES

EPA-BEN 138/07/GT

Porto-Novo, le 23 avril 2007

A qui de droit

Objet : Attestation de recherche

Madame, Monsieur,

Je soussigné, Monsieur Gérard TOGNIMASSOU, Coordonnateur de la Formation et de la Recherche à l'Ecole du Patrimoine Africain -EPA, délivre cette attestation de recherche au Docteur Yannick Saint-Jean, chercheur en anthropologie culturelle, dans le cadre de ses recherches postdoctorales sur « **L'imaginaire catholique au Bénin** » , du **23 avril 2007 au 00 ....2007.**

A cet effet, je vous saurai gré des facilités que vous voudrez bien lui offrir pour l'aboutissement heureux de ses investigations sur le terrain.

Au cours de son séjour, Docteur Yannick Saint-Jean, en plus de ses investigations sur le terrain, animera des séminaires, cours et échanges scientifiques intéressant son domaine de compétence.

Je vous prie de croire, Madame, Monsieur, à l'expression de ma considération distinguée.

Gérard TOGNIMASSOU
Coordonnateur Pôle « Formations et Recherches »

B.P. 2205 Porto-Novo
Bénin

Tél. : (229) 20 21 48 38
Fax : (229) 20 21 21 09
epa@epa-prema.net
http://www.epa-prema.net

REPUBLIQUE DU BENIN
.=.=.=.=.

MINISTERE DE L'ENSEIGNEMENT
SUPERIEUR ET DE LA RECHERCHE
SCIENTIFIQUE
.=.=.=.=.

CABINET DU MINISTRE
.=.=.=.=.

N° 4554 /MESRS/DC/SGM/SA

Cotonou, le 12 novembre 2007

AUTORISATION DE RECHERCHE

Le Ministre de l'Enseignement Supérieur et de la Recherche Scientifique autorise Madame Yanick ST JEAN, Ph.D en Sociologie, chercheur et universitaire de nationalité américaine, professeur de sociologie à l'Institut Jean Paul II de Philosophie et des Sciences Humaines, à effectuer des recherches sur l'imagination catholique à Cotonou, Porto-Novo, Ouidah, Abomey, Parakou, Natitingou.

En foi de quoi, la présente autorisation lui est délivrée pour servir et valoir ce que de droit.

Pour le Ministre de l'Enseignement

Supérieur et de la Recherche Scientifique & P.O

Le Secrétaire Général du Ministère,

Célestin MONTEIRO

CONSENTEMENT

Je, soussigné (e)_____participe
volontairement à cette étude de l'imagination Catholique - un point de vue qui considère
le monde comme imprégné de la présence divine et de l'amour divin, et qui a donc des
conséquences pour le comportement des croyants. Cette imagination Catholique
s'exprimera différemment dans différentes sociétés. D'où cette étude dont le but est de
comprendre l'imagination Catholique Béninoise et ses conséquences pour le
comportement des croyants.

J'autorise Yanick St. Jean à enregistrer mon interview qui durera un maximum de deux
heures. Je comprends que mes réponses seront utilisées seulement pour cette étude après
quoi elles seront détruites. Je comprends aussi que je ne serai pas identifié (e) sans mon
consentement, que je peux me retirer de cette étude a n'importe quel moment, que toute
précaution sera prise pour protéger ma confidentialité et que les conséquences
psychologiques de ma participation seront minimales. En cas de questions, ou si je
voudrais plus d'information, je peux prendre contact avec Yanick St. Jean, Institut
Pontifical Jean Paul II, 04BP 1217, Sce : 21303297, Cotonou]]

Date :

Signatures

Glossary

Aguda: a person of mixed origins, Someone whose skin color is lighter than the general Beninese population.

Analogical imagination: this term is used interchangeably with Catholic imagination and sacramental imagination. See sacramental imagination.

Bidonville: shanty town.

Bokonon: traditional medicine man.

Catholic imagination: this term is used interchangeably with analogical imatination and sacramental imagination. See sacramental imagination.

Divine in the World: this is the same as God in the world and is a characteristic of the sacramental imagination.

Évêque: Bishop.

Envoûtement: belief that one has been hurt by sorcery.

Fon-gbe: language of the Fon people.

Kola: a nut often used in religious ceremonies.

Sacramental imagination: this term refers to seeing "the invisible in the visible," the sacred in the profane (or everyday). Here, the word "imagination" refers to creativity. Think of the sacramental imagination as a religious culture, a Catholic culture or point of view, a sacramental way of seeing the world.

Vodun: traditional African religion practiced primarily in the Southern portion of Benin. Occasionally referred to in this work as Vaudou, or Vodou. I avoid the stigmatized spelling Voodoo.

Yovo: usually refers to a European or white person, but sometimes foreigner regardless of color.

Zemidjans: motor-taxis

Bibliography

Addison, James Thayer. 1924. Ancestor Worship in Africa. *The Harvard Theological Review* 17: 155-171.

Adepoju Aderanti. 1999. *The African family: Demographic policies and Development.* Paris: Karthala.

Adokounou, Barthélemy. 1979. *jalons pur une théologie africaine: essai d'une herméneutique chrétienne du Vodun dahoméen (tome II: étude éthnologique)* Paris: Éditions Lethielleux.

Alladaye, Jérome. 2006. Le *Catholicisme dans le pays du vodou.* Cotonou, Bénin: Les Éditions du Flamboyant.

Allport, Gordon. 1954. *The Nature of Prejudice.* Boston: Beacon.

Appleby, Scott, R. 2000. *The Ambivalence of the Sacred. Religion, Violence, and Reconciliation.* Lanham, MD: Rowman & Littlefield.

Ammerman, Nancy T. 2006. *Everyday Religion: Observing Modern Religious Life.* London: Oxford.

Badufle, G. 1999. Dynamiques religieuses et urbanization dans les campagnes de l'entre-deux villes Cotonou/Porto Novo. Sud-Bénin l'Axe Djeregbé/Kétonou. Mémoire de maitrise de géographie, Université de Caen.

Bamunoba, Y.K. and B. Adoukonou. 1979. *La mort dans la vie africaine: la conception de la mort dans la vie africaine.* Présence Africaine. Paris: Unesco.

Barnes, Sandra T (ed.). 1989. *Africa's Ogun: Old World and New.* Bloomington and Indianapolis: Indiana University Press.

Battle-Waters, K. 2004. *Sheila's Shop: Working class African Americqan Women Talk about Love, Race and Hair.* Lanham, MD: Rowman & Littlefield.

Bellegarde-Smith, Patrick (ed.). 2005. *Fragments of Bone: Neo-African Religions in a New World.* Urbana and Chicago: University of Illinois.

Benjamin, Lois. 2006. *The Black Elite: Still Facing the Color-Line in the Twenty-First Century.* Lanham, MD: Rowman & Littlefield.

Bierman, Alex. 2006: Does Religion Buffer the effects of Discrimination on Mental Health? Differing Effects by Race. *Journal of Scientific Study of Religion* 45: 551-565.

Brekhus, Wayne. 1998. *A Sociology of the Unmarked: Redirecting our Focus.* Sociological Theory 16: 34-51.

Bonilla-Silva, Eduardo. 2006. *Racism Without Racists.* Lanham, MD: Rowman and Littlefield.

Brown, Karen McCarthy. 1989. :Systematic Remembering, Systematic Forgetting: Ogou in Haiti, in Africa's Ogun: Old World and New edited by Sandra T. Barnes. Bloomington and Indiana: Indiana University.

Buchanan, Susan Huelsebusch. 1979. Language and Identity: Haitians in New York City. *International Migration Review* 13: 298-313.

Cipriani, Roberto. 2004. *Manuel de sociologie de la religion*. Paris: L'Harmattan.

Corbett, Bob. http://www.webster.edu/~corbetre/haiti/haiti.html

Cornille Catherine. 2003. Double Religious Belonging. *Buddhist-Christian Studies.* 23: 43-49.

Cox, Roland Paul. 2006. *Parakalew in Hebrews 3:13*. Masters Thesis, Dallas Theological Seminary.

Deren, Maya. 1953. *Divine Horsemen: The Living Gods of Haiti*. London and New York: Thames and Hudson.

Desmangles, Leslie G. 1992. *The Faces of the Gods: Vodou and Roman Catholicism in Haiti*. Chapel Hill: University of North Carolina.

Droogers, André. 2005. Syncretism and Fundamentalism: In Comparison. *Social Compass*. 52: 453-462.

Du Bois, W.E.B. 1969. The *Souls of Black Folk*. New York: New American Library.

Eckert, Andreas; Adams Jones. 2002. Everyday Life in Colonial Africa. *Journal of African Cultural Studies* 15: 5-16.

Emerson, Michael, O. 2006. *People of the Dream*. Princeton, New Jersey: Princeton University Press.

Fandrich, Ina Johanna. 2005. *The Mysterious Voodoo Queen Marie Laveaux: A Study of Powerful Female Leadership in Nineteenth-Century New Orleans*. New York and London: Routledge.

Feagin, Joe R., and Clairece Booher Feagin. 1999. *Racial and Ethnic Relations*. Upper Saddle River, NJ: Prentice.

Feagin, Joe R, Anthony M. Orum and Gideon Sjoberg. 1991. *A Case for the Case Study*. Chapel Hill: University of North Carolina.

————.1975. *Subordinating the Poor*. New Jersey: Prentice.

————. 1968. Black Catholic in the United States. *Sociological Analysis* 29: 186-192.

————. 1964. Prejudice and Religious Types. *Journal of Scientific Study of Religion* 4: 3-13.

Fils-Aimé, Jean 2007. *Vodou, je me souviens: le combat d'une culture pour sa survie*. Québec, Montréal: Éditions Dabar.

Frazier, E. Franklin. 1963. *The Negro Church in America*. USA: The University of Liverpool.

Frazier, E. Franklin. 1939. *The Negro Family in the United States*. Chicago: University of Chicago.

Greeley, Andrew. 2000. *The Catholic Imagination*. Berkeley: University of California.

————. 1991. On Validating David Tracy. *Theology and Sociology* 59: 643-652.

————. 1989. Protestant and Catholic: Is the Analogical Imagination Extinct. *American Sociological Review* 54: 485-502.

Green, Dan S. and Ewin D. Driver. (eds) 1978. *On Sociology and the Black Community*. London: University of Chicago.

Greggus, David, review of *The Faces of Gods: Vodou and Roman Catholicism in Haiti*, by Leslie G. Desmangles. *Hispanic American Historical Review* 74: 172-173.

Guliani, Maurice, s.j. 1997. Trouver Dieu en toutes choses. *Christus*. 174 HS: 200-242.

Herkovits, Melville J. 1939. Dahomey. *The Journal of Negro Education* 8: 209-212.

————. 1937. African Gods and Catholic Saints in New World Negro Belief. *American Anthropologist*, New Series 39: 635-643.

————.1933. On the Provenience of New World Negroes. *Social Forces* 12: 247-262.

Http://en.wikipedia.org/wiki/*Catholic_imagination*.

Idowu, Bolaji E. 1973. *African Traditioinal Religion: A Definition*. N.Y. : Orbis Books.

Iroko, A. Félix. 2003. *La côte des Esclaves et la traite atlantique: Les faits et le jugement de l'histoire*. Cotonou, Bénin: Nouvelle Presse.

Kelly, William S.J. 2000. *Black Catholic Theology: A Sourcebook*. New York: McGraw-Hill.

Law, Robin. 1991. *The slave Coast of West Africa, 1550-1750: The impact of the Atlantic Slave Trade on an African Society*. Oxford: Clarendon.

Levine, Laurence W. 1997. Slave Songs and Slave Consciousness: An Exploration of Neglected Sources. In Furlop/Raboteau, 1997 *African American Religion* pages 58-87.

Lovejoy, Paul E, review of *The slave Coast of West Africa, 1550-1750: The impact of the Atlantic Slave Trade on an African Society*, by Robin Law, *Canadian Journal of African Studies/Revue Canadienne des Études Africaines* 28: 327-328.

Lukes, Steven. 1972. *Émile Durkheim: His Life and Work, a Historical and Critical Study*. Great Britain: Penguin.

Madhavan, Sangeetha. 2001. Female Relationships and Demographic Outcomes in Sub-Saharan Africa. *Sociological Forum* 16: 503-527.

Mann, Kristin, 2007. *Slavery and the Birth of an African City, Lagos, 1760-1900*. Bloomington and Indianapolis: Indiana University.

————.and Ena G. Bay. 2001. *Rethinking the African Diaspora: The Making of a Black Atlantic World in the Bight of Benin and Brazil*. London and Portland OR: Frank Cass.

Maritain, Jacques. 1958. *Reflections on America*. New York: Scribner's Sons.

McNally, Michael, D. 2000. The Practice of Native American Christianity. *Church History* 69: 834-869.

Melville J. Herskovits, 1933. On the Provenience of New World Negroes. *Social Forces* 12: 247-262.

Métraux, Alfred. 1958. *Le vaudou haïtien*. Paris: Éditions Gallimard.

Iroko, A. Félix. 2003. *La côte des esclaves et la traite atlantique: Les faits et le jugement de l'histoire*. Bénin: Nouvelle Presse.

Parés, Luis Nicolau. 2007. Flux et Reflux entre le Bénin et le Brésil: Histoire et présent des religions afro-brésiliennes. Centre International de Conférence. (Bénin, Afrique de l'Ouest) (19 Novembre).

Parrinder, Geoffrey. 1976. *African Traditional Religion*. Wesport, Connecticut: Greenwood.

————.1960. The Religious Situation in West Africa. *African Affairs* 59 38-42.

————.1959. Islam and West African Indigenous Religion. *Numen* 6: 130-141.

Publications du Sillon Noir. 1998. *Le Sillon Noir S'Éxplique*. No 13: 98 Bénin, Cotonou (Janvier).

Rey, Terry. 2005. Habitus et hybridité: une interprétation du syncrétisme dans la religion afro-catholique d'après Bourdieu. *Social Compass* 52: 453-462.

Quénum, André.2007. Personal Communication.

Quénum, André and Yanick St. Jean. 2008. Liturgical Songs and the Catholic Imagination. Paper Presented at the Association for the Sociology of Religion. Boston,
Massachussetts (August).

Rigaud, Marie-Claude Saint-Jean. 2009. Personal Communication.

Rigaud, André. 2010. Personal Communication.

Rockquemore, Kerry Ann and Tracey A Laszloffy. 2008. *The Black Academic Guide to
Winning Tenure Without Losing your Soul*. Boulder: CO: Lynne Rienner.

Sansaricq, Archbishop Guy, 2005. Personal Communication.

Segurola, B. and J. Rassinoux. 2000. *Dictionnaire Fon-Français*. Cotonou, Bénin:
Société des Missions Africaines.

ShawTaylor Yoku and Steven Tuch, eds. 2007. *Other African Americans: Contemporary
African and Caribbean Immigrants in the United States*. Laham: Rowman and
Littlefield.

Slevin, Kathleen and C. Ray Wingrove. 1998. *From Stumbling Blocks to Stepping Stones:
The Life Experiences of Fifty Professional African American Women*. N.Y: New
York University.

Stark, Rodney and Roger Finke. 2000. *Acts of Faith: Explaining the Human Side of Religion*. Berkeley: University of California.

St. Jean, Yanick. 2008. Réinventer le Credo? Note de Recherche sur le Catholicisme
Populaire au Bénin—L'idéal du libre choix. Paper Presented at the International
Conference on Multiculturalism, Democracy and Development in West Africa:
Challenges and Perspectives, Cotonou, Bénin (June).

———. 2008. Réinventer le Credo? Note de Recherche sur le Catholicisme Populaire
au Bénin—L'idéal du libre choix. International Conference on Multiculturalism,
Democracy and Development in West Africa: Challenges and Perspectives, Cotonou, Bénin (Conference Proceedings forthcoming).

———. 2007. Contrasting Religious Preferences between Catholic African Americans
and Haitian Americans. In *The Other African Americans: Contemporary African
and Caribbean Immigrants to the United States*, eds. Yoku-Shaw Taylor and Steven
Tuch, 153-175. Laham, MD: Rowan and Littlefield.

———.and Joe R. Feagin. 1998. *Double Burden: Black Women and Everyday Racism*.
New York: M.E. Sharpe.

Tippet, Krista and Patrick Bellegarde-Smith. 2008. Speaking of Faith: Living Vodou.
Journal of Haitian Studies 14: 144-156.

Triaca, B. 1997. *Itinéraires au Bénin: histoire, art, culture*. Milan: Stéfanoni.

Waters, Mary. 1992. The Process of Ethnogenesis among Haitian and Isreali Immigrants
in the United States. *Ethnic and Racial Studies*.

Wutnow, Robert. 1994. *Sharing the Journey: Support Groups and America's New Quest
for Community*. N.Y.: Free Press.

Zéphir, Flore. 1996. *Haitian Immigrants in Black America: A Sociological and Sociolin-
guistic Portrait*. Westport, CT: Bergin and Garvey.

About the Author

Yanick St. Jean, PhD is the author of several book chapters, journal articles, and the book *Double Burden: Black Women and Everyday Racism* (with Joe Feagin).